Samuel James Watson

**The Constitutional History of Canada**

Samuel James Watson

**The Constitutional History of Canada**

ISBN/EAN: 9783337188344

Printed in Europe, USA, Canada, Australia, Japan

Cover: Foto ©Suzi / pixelio.de

More available books at **www.hansebooks.com**

# THE
# CONSTITUTIONAL
# HISTORY OF CANADA

# THE CONSTITUTIONAL HISTORY OF CANADA.

BY

SAMUEL JAMES WATSON,

LIBRARIAN LEGISLATIVE ASSEMBLY OF ONTARIO.

VOLUME I.

TORONTO:
ADAM, STEVENSON & COMPANY.
1874.

Entered according to the Act of the Parliament of Canada, in the year One Thousand Eight Hundred and Seventy-three, by SAMUEL JAMES WATSON, in the office of the Minister of Agriculture.

HUNTER, ROSE & CO.,
Printers and Binders, Toronto.

# TABLE OF CONTENTS.

### CHAPTER I.
The Capitulation of Canada, 1760—Social condition of the people ... 9

### CHAPTER II.
Royal Proclamation of 1763—Introduction of the Laws of England ... 16

### CHAPTER III.
The French and British desire a House of Assembly ... 22

### CHAPTER IV.
The British Government refuse Canada a House of Assembly—Class Legislation—The Quebec Bill of 1774 ... 27

### CHAPTER V.
Canada and the Thirteen Colonies protest against the Quebec Bill ... 37

### CHAPTER VI.
Dissatisfaction of the majority of the French Canadians—American overtures and invasion ... 46

### CHAPTER VII.
Antagonism of Seignior and Peasant—The Peasants refuse Military service to the Seigniors ... 53

TABLE OF CONTENTS.

## CHAPTER VIII.
The Status of the Roman Catholic Church—The Peasants refuse it political obedience ... ... ... ... 57

## CHAPTER IX.
Peril of the Province—American attack on Quebec—Defeat and expulsion of the Invaders ... ... ... ... 62

## CHAPTER X.
Colonial Misgovernment — French Canadian Legislative Councillors oppose *Habeas Corpus* ... ... .. 66

## CHAPTER XI.
Revival of the French Laws—Nature of these Laws 70

## CHAPTER XII.
Laws of Inheritance—Detestation of Primogeniture ... 74

## CHAPTER XIII.
Feudal Tenure—Peasant Servitudes .. 77

## CHAPTER XIV.
The Canadian Reign of Terror ... ... ... 82

## CHAPTER XV.
Peace between Great Britain and the United States—Its effects on Canada ... .. ... ... .. 87

## CHAPTER XVI.
The people entreat for Constitutional Government—Opposition of the Legislative Council—Deplorable condition of Canada ... .. ... ... ... ... 89

## CHAPTER XVII.
The Nation-Builders of Upper Canada... ... ... ... 93

CONTENTS.

### CHAPTER XVIII.
Canada in the British Parliament—The King's Message ... 97

### CHAPTER XIX.
British Merchants in Eastern Canada oppose the new Bill ... 102

### CHAPTER XX.
Fox and Pitt on the New Constitution ... ... ... 107

### CHAPTER XXI.
The Constitutional Act, 1791 ... ... ... ... ... 116

### CHAPTER XXII.
The defects of the Constitutional Act ... ... ... 126

### CHAPTER XXIII.
The First Parliament of Upper Canada—Abolition of Negro Slavery... ... ... ... ... ... ... ... 130

### CHAPTER XXIV.
The gift of Religious Liberty to Canada ... ... ... 137

### CHAPTER XXV.
Canada Past and Present... ... ... ... ... ... 140

INDEX ... .. ... ... ... ... ... ... 145

THE

# CONSTITUTIONAL HISTORY OF CANADA.

## CHAPTER I.

THE CAPITULATION OF CANADA, 1760 : SOCIAL CONDITION OF THE PEOPLE.

IN camp, before Montreal, September 8, 1760, the Empire of France in North America melted away in fifty-five Articles of Capitulation.* Of these Articles, the twenty-seventh was, as it were, the anchor by means of which the battered barque of the French Canadian race, tossing about on the perilous sea of change, found bottom, grappled and floated.

In this Article, Vaudreuil requested "the free exercise of the Catholic, Apostolic, Roman religion." He asked, further, " that the people shall be obliged by the English

---

\* "Annual Register," 1760, pp. 230. Great Britain was represented by General Amherst, France by the Marquis of Vaudreuil. "The peace of Aix-la-Chapelle (18th Oct., 1748) between England and France, could not be said to extend to the colonies. . . . The ink of the treaty was not dry when the French took possession of the mouth of the river St. John. Nevertheless, in 1750, commissioners from both nations met to try and agree upon a frontier—but in vain. The French Government persisted in the preposterous pretension to connect their possessions in Canada with those of Louisiana by a chain of forts which were to shut out the English from the vast region beyond, and impede trade and communication."—Crowe, "History of France," vol. iv. p. 258.

Government to pay to the priests the tithes and all the taxes they were used to pay under the Government of His Most Christian Majesty."

To these proposals Amherst replied—"Granted, as to the free exercise of their religion. The obligation of paying the tithes to the priests will depend on the King's pleasure." *

The British General, in adjudicating on the Articles of Capitulation, refused to deal with the question of the future government of Canada. He confined himself to the pledging of the faith of Great Britain for full religious liberty, which is amongst the noblest of natural and acquired rights, and the source and fountain of them all.

After the Capitulation, the formative pressure of military rule began to work on Canada. But the system, which lasted about four years, was never before nor since so tenderly administered.†

From 1760 to 1763, the British conquest of Canada was a military, not a diplomatic fact. But, at Paris, on the 10th of February, 1763, in the terms of the fourth clause of the Treaty of Peace, the King of France, amongst other con-

---

* The legal right of the French Canadian clergy to the tithes was granted to them fourteen years afterwards by the Quebec Act (1774).

† In 1773, ten years after the abolition of military law, the Seigniors, a class, of course, apart from the rest of the people of Canada, in a petition to the King of England complained that a civil government, based on the laws of England, had succeeded to the military rule. See the "Maseres Papers," p. 113. [Maseres had been Attorney-General of the province from September 1766 to September 1769; afterwards he was created in England Cursitor-Baron of the Exchequer. He stands, for many reasons, high above the Anglo-Canadian officials of his time. He was the warm and constant friend of the policy of giving to Canada a constitutional government.]

cessions, "ceded and guaranteed to His Britannic Majesty, in full right, Canada, with all its dependencies." *

King George the Third, on his part, "agreed to grant the liberty of the Catholic religion to the inhabitants of Canada. He would consequently give the most precise and most effectual orders that his new Roman Catholic subjects might profess the worship of their religion, according to the rites of the Romish Church, as far as the laws of Great Britain permitted." †

To the storm and alarm of the conquest, there succeeded, for the people of Canada, a calm, unbroken by war, and full of peace and promise. To the peasant-inhabitants, who composed the vast majority of the population, the change of rulers was a blessing palpable and permanent. At the time of the Conquest, the seigniors and the peasants constituted two important factors in the problem of a new Government. The seigniors were entitled, according to the code of feudalism, to erect courts, and to preside in them as judges. They could administer what was known as "haute, moyenne et basse justice." ‡ They could take cognizance of all crimes committed within their jurisdiction, except murder and trea-

* See "Chalmers' Collection of Treaties," vol. i. pp. 476–494.
† The nominal military law in Canada ceased with the consummation of the treaty of peace between Great Britain and France. The continuance of the law was co-existent with the hostility between the two powers. It seems to have been sanctioned more as a precaution against a possible demonstration by the Canadians on behalf of France while at war with Great Britain, than as an active instrument of government. During its continuance, the French laws, in all civil cases, were administered by French Canadians. See the "Maseres Papers," page 113.
‡ "Superior, Ordinary and Inferior Justice."

son.* If they did not, in the French period, exercise their tyrannous rights over the lives, limbs and liberties of their vassals, it was because they were too poor to organize the machinery of Seigniorial Courts, build dungeons and retain jailors and executioners. † That it was this power to crush, which was wanting to the seigniors, and not the spirit, may be seen in their complaint of the hardship of not being permitted, under British rule, to exercise their feudal jurisdiction.‡

The peasant owed compulsory military service to the king; to the seignior, crushing feudal obligation. The Crown was the upper, the lord was the nether millstone, between which the French-Canadian vassal was ground down into a bellicose, tax-paying atom, whirling all his life round the camps pitched against the thirteen British Colonies, and round the coffers of his masters. But, with the Conquest, the peasant came within the rim, and was destined, ere long, to come under the ample centre of the shield of the British Constitution. He was no longer liable to be dragged from his wilderness-farm, to make war, hundreds of miles away, in the wilds of the distant West, on the Frontiersmen of the British Colo-

* Bouchette, "History of Can." vol. i. p. 377.

† Maseres, p. 162. The expenses of a Seigniorial Court would for the most part, have exceeded the whole value of the Seigniory. The average value of the Seigniories, in the French period, did not amount to more than fifty or sixty pounds stg. per annum. "The rich society of the Priests of St. Sulpicius, of Montreal, who are owners of the whole Island of Montreal, besides several other Seigniories," drew an income of more than £4,000 stg. a year. (This was written in 1775.

‡ Maseres Papers, p. 163

nies.* The feudal curb of the seignior was taken out of the vassal's mouth, broken, and cast away for ever. The beak and talons of the Crown were plucked from the breast of the wasted husbandman. He was no longer compelled, by a mandate of the Intendant, issued beforehand, to sell in the market, at a fixed price, the hardwon products of his farm.†

At the time of the conquest, the population was above 65,000 souls.‡ That portion of it which was "noble", in the phrase of heraldry, was represented by about twenty-two families.§ Some of these nobles possessed seigniories; but they were absentees eleven months in the year. The other fractional part they employed in a flying visit devoted to the sweeping up of their feudal dues. The peasants looked upon their lords in the light of tax-gatherers, wringing money out of labour, to spend it in luxury in Quebec and Montreal. The feeling of the peasants towards their seigniors was fear, not affection. This experience, however, is as wide as the circuit of Europe, and as old as feudalism. In the injuries done to

* See, in "Cavendish Debates on the Quebec Bill," the evidence of Governor Carleton, page 105. He stated before the committee of the House of Commons, "Under the French the spirit of the government was military, and conquest was the chief object; very large detachments were sent up every year to the Ohio, and other interior parts of the continent of North America. This drew them from their land, prevented their marriages, and great numbers of them perished. . . . . Since the conquest they have enjoyed peace and tranquillity."

† See "Maseres Papers," page 140, where it is stated the inhabitants of the towns deemed it a great misfortune that the peasant was allowed to sell his products at the highest price he could obtain. The Intendant was an officer whose duty it was to manage the matters of finance, police and justice.

‡ Statement of Quebec Act, 1774.

§ "Maseres Papers," pp 164-168.

him by his seignior, the Canadian peasant could only suffer; redress he had none.* The people who were not "noble," and who were more than 999 out of a thousand, were well pleased that the battering-ram of the Common Law had broken down the fortress of unjust privilege which, in the period of French domination, had walled in the noble from the consequences of his acts.

But it was only in what may be styled his personal and political status, and his release from war-service, that the Canadian peasant was a gainer. The new rule did not emancipate him from the thraldom of feudal obligations in respect to the tenure of his land. Nearly a century after the conquest, † Canada, at the imperative bidding of justice and necessity, was compelled to lift from the peasant's shoulders and to place upon her own, the crushing burden of feudalism, mountainous with the accumulated evils of centuries.

In old France, long before and some time after the Conquest, the nobility abounded in multitudes. Like so many social locusts, they swarmed upon and devoured every green thing.‡ But there was not found prey for them all. Many of them, elbowed out of France, were driven into Canada. § Their functions, in its military

---

* "Mascres Papers," pp. 108–109.
† 1854.
‡ See Crowe, "History of France,' vol. 4, p. 157.
§ Abbé Saint Pierre, quoted in the "Mascres Papers," pp. 159, 160, and writing about the year 1740, estimated the number of noble families in France at no less than 50,000. Mascres, on this computation, reckons the number of noble persons in France—men, women and children—at not less than 250,000, or, perhaps, 300,000. "Many of these," Mascres adds, "it may well be imagined, are miserably poor."

government, were little better than those of titled campfollowers. Some of them, however, were brave soldiers ; many of them fattened on favouritism. British rule meant, for this class, loss of military employment, enforced idleness, or honest labour.* Many of them understood the signs of the times, took advantage of the terms of capitulation, sold out their properties and returned to France. †

It is matter of historical interest that it was in Canada, so long the colony of the hot-bed of European aristocracy, where first that family of feudal fungi were thinned out by new husbandmen, and by the force and pressure of the times. § This event, of such far-reaching import to the future growth of the oft-imperilled germ of our political liberties, was one of the most vital results of the Conquest.

* By the French feudal law, a nobleman who engaged in trade forfeited his patent of nobility.

† "Maseres," p. 170, says : " The English Government was happily rid of that part of the inhabitants of this new acquired Province who were most likely to be discontented under it." The Abbé Raynal, quoted by "Maseres," p. 171, speaks much more severely of the nobles in Canada. He styles them "these despicable creatures" (ces êtres méprisables). He asks if the colony has not gained immensely in being relieved of all these lazy nobles who had fastened themselves upon it for so long a time—of these insolent nobles who, in Canada, entertained contempt for all sorts of labour ?

§ Governor Carleton in 1774, ("Cavendish Debates," p. 107), when asked what number of noblesse was in the country, said his memory would not suffer him to tell. He supposed a hundred and fifty ; but he said he spoke at random. Maseres, who puts the number of families at twenty-two, was much more likely to be right in his estimate.

# CHAPTER II.

ROYAL PROCLAMATION, 1763; INTRODUCTION OF TH_
LAWS OF ENGLAND.

On the 7th of October, 1763, the year of the Treaty of Paris, the King of Great Britain put forth a Royal Proclamation.* It announced that he had granted letters patent, under the great seal, to erect Quebec into a Government. It also defined the boundaries of that Province.†

The proclamation asserted that the King had given "express power and direction" to the Governor, "that, so soon as the state and circumstance of the colony would admit thereof, * * * the Governor should summon and call a General Assembly." It was, furthermore, solemnly promised that, " until such Assembly can be called, * * *

---

\* See "Annual Register, 1763," pp. 208, 213.

† As the next definition of the boundary of Quebec, in 1774, played a momentous part in the disputes between Great Britain and her thirteen colonies, it may be interesting in this place to give the boundary as laid down by the proclamation :—

Quebec was to be bounded on the Labrador Coast by the River St. John (Saguenay); thence by a line drawn from the head of that river through Lake St. John to the south end of Lake Nipissim; whence the line, crossing the St. Lawrence and Lake Champlain in 45 degrees of N. latitude, passed along the High Lands which divide the rivers that empty themselves into the St. Lawrence from those that fall into the sea; thence sweeping along the North coast of the Baie des Chaleurs, and the coast of the Gulf of St. Lawrence to Cap Rosieres, the line crossed the mouth of the St. Lawrence by the West end of the Island of Anticosti, and terminated at the aforesaid River St. John.

all persons inhabiting in, or resorting to, our said colony may confide in our Royal protection for the enjoyment of the benefit of the laws of our realm of England." In the commission to General Murray, appointing him Captain-General and Governor-in-chief of Quebec, and in the commission of his successor, General Carleton, the King repeated the promise of the proclamation.

In the commissions to the Governors Murray and Carleton, the King directed that the members of the future Assembly should take the oaths appointed by the statute of 1st George the First. These oaths presented a strange commixture of secular obligation and religious dogma. There was the oath of allegiance; the oath of abjuration of the Pope's authority; the oath of abjuration of the Pretender's right to the crown. In addition, the member of the future Assembly was required "to make and subscribe the declaration against transubstantiation."*

The King, in his instructions to the Governors, declared that until an Assembly should be summoned, a Council was to be appointed to assist in certain of the lesser duties of legislation. For the appointment of this Council there was no authority in the commission of the Governor, which commission was issued under the great seal of Great

---

* "Maseres Papers," page 42. Of these oaths there were two, or at least there was one, which no conscientious Roman Catholic could prevail upon himself to take. This being the case, the French Canadians could hope for no representation in the promised Assembly by men of their own faith. In 1764, an Assembly of delegates from all the parishes except Quebec was called, but never sat; for the Canadian members, as Roman Catholics, could not take the oaths. Bouchette, "History of Canada," vol. 1, p. 441. The oaths were abolished by the Quebec Act of 1774.

Britain. The instrument directing him to appoint the Council was issued under the King's "Royal Signet and Sign Manual." *

The Governor and Council were empowered under the "Royal Signet and Sign Manual" to advance, as it were, a step beyond the threshold of legislation. They were invested with "an authority to make such rules and regulations as should appear to be necessary for the peace, order and good government of the province: taking care that nothing be passed or done that shall any ways tend to affect the life, limb or liberty of the subject, or to the imposing any duties or taxes." †

This epoch was one of experiment and transition. Two different systems of language, religion and social order were revolving round a common centre—the King of Great Britain. The orbits of these systems intercrossed: sometimes collision threatened: often doubt and fear were the result. The Canadian noblesse were much dissatisfied with the British mode of trial; not with the dealing out of justice. The expenses of the new laws frightened them. They detested juries. They could not under-

---

\* "Maseres Papers," p. 43. The Baron raises, pp. 44–45, an interesting constitutional issue. He doubts "whether a power of this kind could be legally communicated to the Governor by any other instrument than letters patent under the Great Seal of Great Britain, publicly read and notified to the people, to the end that the acts done by virtue of them may have a just claim to obedience." As to private instructions to the Governor, the people were not assured whether they had been received or not. In such case the people "cannot presume that he (the Governor) acts by his Majesty's authority, and therefore are not bound to obey him."

† "Maseres Papers," page 43.

stand why the British in Canada would rather have matters of law decided by tailors and shoemakers, than by a judge alone.* A Canadian gentleman would have chosen the torture of the rack sooner than be tried by his tradesmen. † The French Canadians detested the inhumanity and injustice of the English law of primogeniture; in this respect they and the British colonists were in harmony. ‡

In the month of April, 1770, there was prepared, by order of Governor Carleton, a statement as to the numbers of the British colonists in the Province of Quebec. He believed the return "included everybody who called himself a Protestant." According to this statement, there were in the whole colony between three hundred and sixty and four hundred men, besides women and children. In 1774 that number had become smaller: the circumstances of the British colonists had been so reduced as to force the people to leave the Province. Of the number of colonists in 1770, there were some who had purchased lands—officers, or reduced officers. There were some respectable merchants. There were engaged in trade a number of inferior officers and disbanded soldiers.

The number of French Canadians amounted to about 150,000 souls—all Roman Catholics. The British co-

* "Debates on the Canada Bill," p. 102. (Evidence of Governor Carleton.) He spoke for the noblesse; not for the rest of the people. See "Maseres," p. 139.

† Attorney-General Thurlow's Report to the King, on the State of Canada, January 22nd, 1773. Quoted in Christie's "Lower Canada," vol. l. pp. 57-58.

‡ "Maseres," pp. 288-289.

lonists and the French Canadians were almost strangers to each other.* A distrust, common to both, infected with its poisoned leaven the whole body politic. The hard, irresistible wedge of race clove and kept them asunder.

The British colonists in Canada, at the end of the year 1773, when looking back on the position they had been made to occupy since 1763, were forced to complain of the treatment they had received from the mother country. From 1763, the year of the Royal Proclamation, they had been trusting, in loyal patience, to the fulfilment of its promise. This promise was that the Governor, as soon as the circumstances of the Colony would permit, should call a General Assembly. Now it was the year 1773, and the Royal promise had not been kept. The result was that the British colonists found themselves, for ten long years, robbed of the protection of their own Constitution.† They were outlaws, without being infamous. They were the subjects, not of the Empire, but of a Governor and Council. For the acts of either, were those acts secretly mischievous or openly tyrannical, the British resident of Canada, unlike the inhabitant of any of the Thirteen Colonies, had no redress. It was no wonder, then, that high-spirited

* "Debates on the Canada Bill," pp. 103, 109.
† So long before, as 1720, Mr. West, Counsel to the Board of Trade, and afterwards Lord Chancellor of Ireland, declared that the Common Law of England was the Common Law of the Colonies. " Let an Englishman go where he will, he carries as much law and liberty with him as the nature of things will bear.' (See Forsyth's " Cases and Opinions of Constitutional Law," p. 1.)

emigrants from the British Islands turned away from Canada, over which Irresponsible Government brooded, blighting like a plague, and set their faces toward the harbours of the freer Thirteen Colonies.

There has now been explored the social quarry, so to speak, out of which were to be raised and fashioned into shape the materials for future Parliaments—diverse materials, destined, perhaps, to rise up, under the workmanship of Time, into a harmonious edifice of free government, upholding a noble and hospitable roof of empire, whose eaves overhang the two oceans.

# CHAPTER III.

### FRENCH AND BRITISH DESIRE A HOUSE OF ASSEMBLY.

In the month of January, 1774, the British colonists in Montreal and Quebec sent to the King a petition, and to the Earl of Dartmouth, Secretary of State for America, a memorial, entreating for a House of Assembly. *

In the month of March, 1774, Baron Maseres presented to the King the petition of the British colonists, and to the Earl of Dartmouth their memorial.† The petition recited the promise of the Royal Proclamation of 1763. Then it asserted that a General Assembly would very much contribute to encourage and promote industry, agriculture and commerce, and, as the petitioners hoped, to create harmony and a good understanding between French and British. In conclusion, the petition left the constitution and form of the General Assembly to the Royal wisdom.

The memorial was in somewhat different terms. It

---

\* The majority of the French were in favour of a House of Assembly. ("Maseres Papers," p. 30.) But, because the British would not petition to throw open the Assembly to Roman Catholic representatives, the French would not join in the petition. (Ibid, p. 40.) The language of the British petition was very far from being straightforward. The truth would seem to be that both races were blameworthy. The British were narrow-minded; the French short-sighted.

† The petition bore 148 names. ("Maseres Papers," p. 131.) The name which occurs oftenest in all the proceedings to obtain a House of Assembly, is that of Zachary Macaulay, father of Great Britain's greatest historian.

stated that the British colonists, encouraged by the Royal Proclamation of 1763, purchased lands, planted, settled, and carried on trade and commerce to a very considerable amount, and to the manifest advantage of Great Britain. These things were done in confident expectation of the early accomplishment of the promise of the Proclamation. The memorialists now prayed the King to relieve them from their fears as to their property being endangered, and as to losing the fruits of their labour. They were afraid of these evils, because they were exposed to the ordinances of a Governor and Council. These ordinances, which were repugnant to the laws of England, were put in force before the King's pleasure was known. And these same ordinances were not only contrary to the King's commission and private instructions to the Governor, but were equally grievous to French and English.

The Ministers of the King of England looked with no friendly eye on the object of the British colonists. Still, there was open to the latter a narrow and miry path by which they might have marched to success. But they refused to tread it.

In a letter from Baron Maseres to the committee of the British colonists, dated March 19, 1774, he informed them that he had presented their petitions. In the same letter he warned them that he knew of nothing that would contribute more to their obtaining a General Assembly than the making of a previous declaration. This declaration was, that every member of such future Assemby, before being permitted to take his seat, should be required to recognize, in the plainest and strongest terms, the supreme authority of the British Parliament in every matter whatsoever, both of legislation and taxation. Such a previous confession of political faith would greatly tend to remove the prejudices in the minds of many people in England against the erection of new Houses of Assembly in America. These prejudices arose "from the conduct of the Assembly in Boston and in others of the American Provinces, in totally denying the supreme authority of Parliament."*

The British colonists, national narrow-mindedness apart, were true to their own old constitution, to Canada and to themselves. They longed for an Assembly; but they chose rather to keep company with that " hope deferred that maketh the heart sick," than to sacrifice on the altar of expediency the principles which were the life, pith and marrow of the British constitution. They felt that a legislative body bound hand and foot in such chains of obligation would be nothing but a crippled changeling, from which the eye and reason of British Islanders would turn away in disgust and in wrathfulness.

About the month of February, 1774, a petition of the French Canadians was presented to the King. Opening

* " Maseres Papers," pp. 35, 87, 88.

with a warm outpour of devotion to the person of His Majesty, the petition proceeded to bear hearty witness to the clemency which followed upon the conquest.* One proof of this clemency was, that the former countrymen of the petitioners were made judges in disputes concerning civil matters. But now the petition turned into the channel of complaint. In 1774, His Majesty thought fit to put an end to the Military Government of the Province, and to establish a Civil Government in its stead. From the moment of this change, the petitioners began to feel the inconveniences that came in with the laws of England, with which, until that time, the French Canadian inhabitants had no acquaintance.† The petition concluded with a most fervent prayer for the restoration of the ancient laws, privileges, and customs of the country:†

* The petition, which represented the aristocratic and legal French Canadian classes, bore 65 names ; the British petition 148. To make up the 65 names, some of the French petitioners caused their children to sign it. The Roman Catholic Bishop and his clergy took "infinite pains to procure the signatures." ("Maseres Papers," pp. 131, 132.)

† The words are—"Dans l'année 1764, votre Majesté daigna faire cesser le gouvernement militaire dans cette colonie, pour y introduire le gouvernement civil. Et dès l'époque de ce changement, nous commençames à nous appercevoir des incouvenients qui résultoient des loix Britanniques, qui nous étoient jusqu'alors inconnues." ("Maseres Papers," p. 113.)

‡ The torture of the rack, in the administration of the French criminal law of Canada, was of common occurrence. (See "Christie's History of Lower Canada," vol. i. p. 11.) The British conquest abolished this diabolical and barbarous practice. But, strange to say, the English ministry were on the point of re-enacting the French criminal law in 1774, and were only prevented by the strong remonstrances of Mr. Hey, Chief Justice of Quebec! (Maseres, p. 231.) In 1774 Governor Carleton believed there were more punishments in the law of England than in the law of Canada, but could not pronounce. ("Debates on Quebec Bill," p. 117.) He might have safely pronounced in favour of Canada--barring the rack. See note to page 34.

B

for the extension of the Province to its former boundaries: for the bestowal of the Royal favours on all the inhabitants without distinction. But not one word nor hint concerning a House of Assembly.

The signers of the petition presented a memorial in its support. The most noteworthy feature of the memorial was its prayer for extension of boundary. It entreated that, as under the French Government, Canada was permitted to extend over all the upper countries known as Michilimakinac, Detroit, and other adjacent places, as far as the River Mississippi, so the colony might now be enlarged to the same extent. The King was also implored to re-annex to the Province the coast of Labrador, which formerly belonged to it, and had been taken from it since the peace. It was represented that the colony was not in a condition to defray the expenses of a General Assembly. A council of a larger representation than heretofore, to be composed partly of British and partly of French, was suggested in preference.

# CHAPTER IV.

THE BRITISH GOVERNMENT REFUSE CANADA A HOUSE OF ASSEMBLY. CLASS LEGISLATION—THE QUEBEC BILL, 1774.

In the House of Lords, on the 2nd of May, 1774, the Earl of Dartmouth introduced a Bill "For making more Effectual Provision for the Government of the Province of Quebec." The measure was founded on the petition of the French noblesse ;* every clause of it showed that the petition of the British colonists had been unjustly and contemptuously rejected. Nor did the Bill recognise the wishes of the majority of the French Canadian people.†
Even in that gloomy epoch of the constitutional history of Great Britain—a time when servile majorities, the

---

* "Maseres Papers," p. 131.

† Governor Carleton, in his examination before the Committee of the House of Commons, stated that an Assembly composed of the British inhabitants would give great offence to the Canadians. He had no doubt they would greatly prefer, to such an Assembly, the rule of a Governor and Legislative Council. Several of the Canadians had told him that Assemblies had drawn upon the other Colonies so much distress, riot, and confusion, that "they wished never to have one of any kind whatever." ("Debates on Quebec Bill," pp. 105-106.) On the other hand, M. de Lotbiniere, a native Canadian nobleman, declared before the Committee that the natural inclination of the Canadians would be to be governed by a Legislature like that of Great Britain, provided they themselves were allowed to be part of it. An Assembly was suitable for Canada. The Canadians would certainly desire a freer government than a Governor with a Council, the members of which he was to appoint, and could remove and suspend. He (M. de Lotbiniere) considered such a Council in no other light than that of a despotism. He believed the people would wish to choose their own Council, and not leave the choice in the hands of the Crown. ("Debates," p. 162.) The weight of belief leans toward M. de Lotbiniere rather than toward the Governor.

pampered Prætorians of the Court, rushed daily to the attack on the citadel of English freedom—this Bill stands conspicuous for the criminal ignorance in which it was conceived, and the perilous rashness in which it had its birth.

The indecent haste with which the Bill was rushed through the House of Lords, showed that the Prime Minister, Lord North, and his colleagues were urged forward by a spur which was then at its sharpest. On the 17th of May the Bill passed the Lords. Tossed, as it were, to the Commons, it came before that House for the second reading on the 26th of May. Here it was opposed by the outnumbered but undaunted band who did battle for the imperilled constitution. Burke, Fox, Colonel Barré, Chas. Townshend jr., Serjeant Glynn, combatted those enactments which proposed to extinguish the rights which British colonists inherited as members of the Island races.*

Lord North, with his Attorney-General Thurlow, and his Solicitor-General Wedderburne, defended the Bill in its most iniquitous clauses.† They voted down an amendment by Mr. Mackworth, to establish trial by jury, in civil cases, at the option of either of the disputing parties.‡ The Government, and its servile horde, next

---

* See " Debates on the Canada Bill," passim. See note, *ante* p. 16, Forsyth's "Constitutional Opinions."

† See " Debates Canada Bill," passim.

‡ " Debates on Canada Bill," pp. 254, 290. Strange to say, this optional system had been in operation for ten years, and worked well. See Mr. Mansfield's speech in " Debates," p. 91. Mr. Mansfield opposed the Bill on behalf of the merchants of London.

trampled down an amendment by Mr. Thos. Townshend, jr., proposing to make temporary that part of the Bill relating to the existence of the Legislative Council, about to be established by the measure.*

The great grievance of this Bill—the one which, in its very nature, was sure to make continuous and calamitous war upon the instincts of every colonist with British blood in his veins—was that it denied to him his native right to the sovereign boon of habeas corpus. Mr. Dempster moved an amendment to provide that the Bill should enact that "the English laws of *habeas corpus*, and of bail in cases of commitment," should prevail in Canada.

The amendment was lost. A motion of the same member, that the proposed Legislative Council should carry on its proceedings in public, was also negatived.

On the 13th of June, the Bill, by a vote of 56 to 20, received its third reading. It was sent back to the House

---

\* "Debates," pp. 290, 291. Mr. Townshend was prepared to move that the term of the existence of the proposed Council should be seven years. Then to establish a Legislative Assembly.

† The opponents of the Bill raised an important constitutional issue as to the proposal to revive the French laws concerning matters of property and civil rights. Mr. Dunning put the matter in this shape: Personal liberty is a civil right; the Bill says that in all matters of property and civil rights, resort shall be had to the laws of Canada, and not to the laws of England. Hence it must follow that if a man were deprived of his liberty by a *lettre de cachet*, and application were made to the Chief Justice of Canada for his discharge, the Chief Justice would be bound to answer that, as this was a matter concerning a civil right, he must proceed by the laws of Canada, which afforded a man no relief when he was imprisoned by the King's *lettres de cachet*. See " Maseres Papers, pp. 228-229."

of Lords, with a few verbal amendments which had been tacked on to it in the Commons.

The Earl of Chatham, trembling, at the time, on the verge of the grave, dragged himself down to the House of Lords, to raise a prophetic warning against the Bill. He proclaimed that "it was a most cruel, oppressive and odious measure, tearing up justice and every good principle by the roots; that the whole of it appeared to him to be destructive of that liberty which ought to be the ground-work of every constitution : and that it would shake the affections and confidence of His Majesty's subjects in England and Ireland, and finally lose him the hearts of all the Americans."* The Earl had only the ear of the Lords; in the case of the majority of that House, the Court had every other faculty they possessed. They passed the Bill : contents, 26 ; non-contents, 7.

On the 22nd of June, the Lord Mayor of London, accompanied by several Aldermen, the Recorder, and upwards of one hundred and fifty of the Common Council, went up with an address and petition to the King. The object was to pray him to refuse his assent to the Bill. The Lord Chamberlain, by order of the King, informed the deputation, that " as the petition related to a Bill agreed on by the two Houses of Parliament, of which His Majesty could not take notice until it was presented for his Royal assent, they were not to expect an answer." The reply had scarcely left the lips of the Lord Cham-

* "Debates," Editor's Preface, pp. iii., iv.

berlain when the King proceeded to the House of Lords to prorogue Parliament. He assented to the Bill; observing that "it was founded on the clearest principles of justice and humanity; and would, he doubted not, have the best effect in quieting the minds and promoting the happiness of his Canadian subjects."*

Thus passed a measure which in its far-reaching, disastrous results was—not even excepting the Stamp Act of 1765, which began to goad the Thirteen Colonies to revolution—the worst Act the British Parliament ever imposed on an American colony.

Not to speak of the feeling on this side the Atlantic, the opinions of the more intelligent portion of the British people were strongly against the measure. The merchants of London appointed Mr. Mansfield to appear before the committee of the Commons to combat the Bill.†

It is probable that this vicious measure had one object in view. It is certain that it had in view a second, to the full as reprehensible as the other. The first seems to have been to throw down the gage of embittered bat-

* "Debates," Editor's Preface, p. iv.
† "Debates," p. 90. One of the grounds the great legist took was, that in a political point of view, as a defence of liberty, it was material that civil as well as criminal causes should be decided by juries. For one of the great checks to arbitrary power was this, that every undue exertion of it to the injury of an individual might be brought to the tribunal of a jury. If Canada were to be enslaved under a Legislative Council, the maintenance of the British jury laws was the more imperatively necessary. For if persons were injured, and no jury laws in existence, they would have no one to whom to apply but to judges holding office at the pleasure of the Governor, and certainly at the pleasure of the Crown.

tle to the discontented Thirteen Colonies. The second object was proclaimed by the lips of Solicitor-General Wedderburne in the debate on the Bill. His words were—" Now, I confess that the situation of the British settler is not the principal object of my attention. I do not wish to see Canada draw from this country any considerable number of her inhabitants. I think there ought to be no temptation held out to the subjects of England to quit their native soil to increase the colonies at the expense of this country. * * With regard to the English who have settled there, their number is very few. They are attached to the country either in point of commercial interest, or they are attached to it from the situations they hold under Government. It is one object of this measure that these persons should not settle in Canada."*

It is now time to show the nature and essence of this memorable Act.

The preamble recited the Royal Proclamation of the 7th of October, 1763; then it declared that in the arrangements made by the Proclamation, " a very large extent of country, within which there were several colonies of the subjects of France, who claimed to remain therein under the faith of the Treaty of Paris, was left without any provision being made for the administration of civil government."

The preamble next proceeded to enact that certain

* "Debates," pp. 57, 58.

immense territories, especially to the west, should be annexed to the Province of Quebec.*

The Act revoked the Royal Proclamation; with the revocation was violated the Royal promise to the British colonists.† The measure then began the work of concession. To the Roman Catholics was granted the free exercise of their religion, subject to the King's supremacy as declared in the first year of Queen Elizabeth. To the Roman Catholic clergy liberty was given "to hold, receive and enjoy their accustomed dues and rights, with respect to such persons only as should profess the said religion."‡

A qualification was appended to this clause: Out of the said "accustomed dues and rights," the King might make such provision, as he might deem expedient, for the support of a Protestant clergy.

To persons professing the Roman Catholic religion,

---

* The enactment is too long to be reproduced here. Bancroft says on the matter, vol. 6, p. 527 : " It (the Bill) extended the boundaries of the (Quebec) Government to the Ohio and the Mississippi : and over the vast region which included, besides Canada, the area of the present States of Ohio, Michigan, Indiana, Illinois and Wisconsin, it extended an arbitrary rule. The Quebec Bill, which quickly passed the House of Lords, and was borne through the Commons by the zeal of the Ministry and the influence of the King, left the people who were to colonize the most fruitful territory in the world without the writ of *habeas corpus* to protect the rights of persons, and without a share in any one branch of the government."

† See *ante*, pp. 12-13 " And until such an Assembly can be called, all persons inhabiting in, or resorting to, our said colony may confide in our Royal protection for the enjoyment of the benefit of the laws of our realm of England."

‡ The dues amounted to one twenty-six part of all grain produced on the farms; and to occasional assessments for building and repairing churches and parsonage-houses, etc. Bouchette, "Hist. Can.," Vol. 1. p. 378. The tithe of the Church of England at the time, was one-tenth.

relief was given in the matter of the oath of 1st Elizabeth.* There was substituted an oath which was simply one of allegiance to the King's person. The refusal to take this modified oath carried with it the penalties of 1st Elizabeth. To the King's French Canadian subjects, religious orders excepted, was extended the right to hold all their possessions in full security.†

In all questions as to property and civil rights, the civil laws of Canada were to decide. But from these laws were exempted lands granted by the King in common soccage.

The criminal law of the Province was to be the code of England. According to the words of the Act, "the certainty and lenity" of the code had been sensibly felt by the inhabitants from an experience of more than nine years.‡

* The object of modifying the oath was to enable Roman Catholics to hold office under the Crown. The oath of 1st. Elizabeth cap. 1st. declared the Queen's ecclesiastical and temporal supremacy. Ecclesiastical and secular office-bearers were compelled to take this oath. The penalties of refusal were deprivation of office ; and permanent disqualification.

† To the credit of the British Government, this provision as to religious orders, except with regard to the Jesuits, remained a dead letter. ("Christie's History of Lower Canada," vol. 1, p. 10.) Not until the last of the Jesuits, Father Casot, died in 1800, were their possessions taken by the Government, and applied to educational purposes. (Ibid. p. 39.) The order of the Jesuits was suppressed in 1773 by Pope Clement XIV., "with their functions, houses and institutions." (Knight, "Hist. Eng.," vol. 6, p. 327.) " In 1764, the Jesuits, or those who persisted in remaining so, were finally banished from France. All the Bourbon courts followed the example." Crowe, "Hist. France," vol. 4, p. 302.

‡ To point out the giant strides which the mother country has taken within the last century, it may be stated that, at the period of the passing of this Act, every line of the English criminal law dripped with blood. May, in his "Constitutional History of England," vol. 3, pp. 393–396, says of the English crimi-

The Act, after having declared "that it is at present inexpedient to call an Assembly," proceeded to authorize the appointment of a Council.

This body was to consist of not more than twenty-three, and not less than seventeen members. It was to have power "to make ordinances for the peace, welfare, and good government of the Province." But it was not authorized to impose taxes or duties within the Province, except for public roads and buildings.

Every ordinance of the Council was, within six months after its passing, to be transmitted to the King for his approbation. The King retained the power to disallow every such ordinance.

No ordinance touching religion, or by which any punishment might be inflicted greater than fine, or imprisonment for three months, was to be of effect until it had received the King's approval.

No ordinance was to be passed where less than a majority of the whole Council was present. No ordinances, except on urgent occasions, were to be passed except be-

nal law of this period—" The lives of men were sacrificed with a reckless barbarity worthier of an Eastern despot or an African chief than of a Christian State. From the Restoration to the reign of George the Third, a period of 160 years, no less than 187 capital offences were added to the criminal code. In the reign of George II. thirty-three Acts were passed creating capital offences; in the first fifty years of George III. no less than sixty-three. Murder became, in the eye of the law, no greater crime than picking a pocket. Such law-makers were as ignorant as they were cruel. Obstinately blind to the evil of their blood-stained laws, they persisted in maintaining them long after they had been condemned by jurists, and by the common sense and humanity of the people. Crime was not checked; but, in the words of Horace Walpole, the country became 'one great shambles:' and the people were brutalized by the hideous spectacle of public executions."

tween the first of January and the first of May. In such case every member at, or within fifty miles of Quebec, was to be personally summoned.

The King reserved the right, whenever he thought it necessary, to constitute courts of criminal, civil and ecclesiastical jurisdiction within the Province.

The Bill, in its last clause, provided that nothing which it contained should be held to repeal, within the Province, any previous Acts of the British Parliament "for prohibiting, restraining, or regulating the trade and commerce of His Majesty's colonies and plantations in America." All such Acts were declared to be in force in every part of the Province of Quebec.

The spirit of the Act may be thus pourtrayed : It confirmed to the French Canadian Roman Catholics the fullest religious liberty; this was most praiseworthy. It restored the old civil laws of the Province; this was liberal. But it extended these laws over the British in Canada, and over five immense territories inhabited by twenty thousand people of British blood; this was unjust. It deprived all these people of trial by jury in civil cases; this was harsh. In their faces it shut the doors of local Parliaments; this was unconstitutional. But, worst of all, the Act robbed the British colonist of Canada, his French Canadian fellow-citizen, and the men of the five incorporated territories, of the sovereign right of *Habeas Corpus;* and this was rank tyranny.

# CHAPTER V.

## CANADA AND THE THIRTEEN COLONIES PROTEST AGAINST THE QUEBEC BILL.

No sooner had the Quebec Act reached Canada, than it was received by the British colonists with a stern dissatisfaction which found vent in resolute remonstrance. These men at once felt the full force of the statement of Mr. Thomas Townshend, jr., when opposing the Bill in the House of Commons. For that clear-headed friend and defender of the Constitution had told the Ministry: " You have given up to Canada almost all that country which was the subject of dispute, and for which we went to war. We went to war calling it the Province of Virginia. You tell the French it was only a pretext for going to war; that you knew then, you know now, that it was part of the Province of Canada."*

The general feeling of alarm † which seized upon the British colonists found expression in earnest public meetings. They prepared, with all speed, a petition to the King; one to the House of Lords; a third to the House of Commons. The petition to the King § opened with a reference to the faith of his " Sacred Majesty's Royal Proclamation." Upon that faith

---

\* See "Debates on Canada Bill," p. 4.
† Maseres Papers, p. 238.
§ It was dated " Quebec, 12th Nov., 1774;" and presented to the King in the month of January, 1775.

British colonists made their homes in Canada. In consequence of this fact, "the value of the land and the wealth of its inhabitants were more than doubled." But by a late Act of Parliament the petitioners " found, and, with unutterable grief presumed to say * * that they were deprived of the franchises granted by His Majesty's Royal predecessors, and by the petitioners inherited from their ancestors."

The evil results of the Act were enumerated. The British colonists had lost the protection of the English laws. In their stead the laws of Canada were to be introduced —" laws to which we are utter strangers, disgraceful to us as Britons, and in their consequences ruinous to our properties, as we thereby lose the invaluable privileges of trial by juries." The writ of *habeas corpus* was " dissolved." In consequence, the petitioners were subjected, " to arbitrary fine and imprisonment at the will of the Governor and Council, who may, at pleasure, render the criminal laws of no effect, by the great power that is granted to them of making alterations in the same."

In conclusion, the petitioners most humbly implored the King to take their unhappy state into consideration, and to grant them such relief as in his royal wisdom he should think meet.

The petition to the House of Lords * was, in substance, similar to the one presented to the King. In the colonial innocence of their hearts, the petitioners concluded in this strain :—

\* The petition bore date, Quebec, Nov. 12, 1774.

"In this cruel state of apprehension and uncertainty, we humbly implore your lordships' favourable interposition, as the hereditary guardians of the rights of the people, that the said Act may be repealed or amended." On the 17th of May, 1775, Lord Camden presented the petition to the House of Lords.* At the same time he introduced a Bill to repeal the Quebec Act. But the Earl of Dartmouth opposed the Bill, and on his motion it was rejected.‡

The petition to the House of Commons was from " His Majesty's ancient subjects, the seigneurs, freeholders, merchants, traders and others settled in His Majesty's Province of Quebec."§

The petition opened with the statement that the Royal Proclamation was the main inducement to British settlement in Canada. Then came the assertion that the country had flourished chiefly through the industry and enterprising spirit of the British colonists. Through their hands passed four parts out of five of all the imports and exports of the country. Their real and personal property was, excluding the possessions of the religious

* "Parliamentary History," Vol. 18, pp. 655—666.
‡ *Ibid.* p. 676. The Contents for the Earl of Dartmouth's motion were 88, non-contents, 28.
§ Maseres Papers, p. 254. In the "Case of the London Merchants trading to Quebec," which, the previous year, had been presented to members of both Houses of Parliament against the passing of the Bill, it was stated that sixteen of the Seigniories of the Province, and some of them the most valuable ones in the country, were in the hands of the British colonists. The same document stated that, in 1773, Canada exported 350,000 bushels of corn ; whereas, in the French period, it exported none at all, and produced hardly enough for its own subsistence. Maseres' Papers, pp. 202—213.

communities, equal to one-half of the whole real and personal valuation of Canada.

The petitioners had observed, with deep concern, that, in a certain examination taken before the House of Commons,\* the British colonists had been grossly abused and misrepresented as well as to their numbers as in their importance in the Province. The number of French Canadians had been greatly exaggerated, for, by the last computation, it was about 75,000. On the other hand, an enumeration of the British showed that at this time they amounted to upwards of 3000 souls.†

The Act had "already struck a damp upon the credit of the country." It had "alarmed all the petitioners with just apprehensions of arbitrary fines and imprisonments." If the Act were carried out, it "would oblige the British to quit the Province, or, in the end, it must accomplish their ruin and impoverish or hurt their generous creditors, the merchants of Great Britain." The petition ended with a prayer for the repeal or amendment of the Act ; that the British colonists might have the benefit of the English laws in so far as related to personal property ; and that their liberty might be ascertained according to their ancient constitutional rights and privileges.

\* The allusion is to the examination of Gov. Carleton and others. See "Debates," pp. 100–169.

† See *ante*, p. 19. Carleton's evidence, as to the number of the British in 1770, seems untrustworthy. But, accepting his figures, the increase to upwards of 3,000 in 1774 is quite comprehensible, if we take into account the disturbed state of the Thirteen Colonies.

CONSTITUTIONAL HISTORY OF CANADA. 41

Sir George Savile, who, on the 18th of May, submitted the petition to the Commons, moved to repeal the Quebec Act.* Lord North, during the debate, made an announcement not calculated to appease the fears to which the Quebec Act had given rise in the Thirteen Colonies. "He stood up in his place to assert that, if the refractory colonies cannot be reduced to obedience by the present forces, he should think it a necessary measure to arm the Roman Catholics of Canada, and to employ them in that service."†

Charles James Fox charged that Lord North "did not choose to own who was the real planner of the Quebec Bill. In withholding from the Canadians an Assembly, and in putting arms in their hands, he (Lord North) showed that he was more afraid of their tongues than of their swords. After Lord North's shameful neglect and procrastination, he (Fox) was convinced that if the disputes had not arisen with our American colonies, the Act of last year would never have been thought of, but the colony left without law or any political regulation whatever."‡ The fate of Lord Camden's motion in the House of Lords the day before, was the fate of Sir George Savile's—it was lost by a large majority.§

But it was not only the British colonists who were grieved and disappointed with the Bill. The French

* "Parliamentary History," Vol. 18, p. 676.
† Ibid. Vol. 18, p. 681.
‡ Ibid, Vol. 18, p. 681.
§ Ibid, p. 684. The numbers were : For, 86 ; against, 174.

C

Canadians in general were displeased with it.* They declared that it was not at their desire or solicitation that it had been passed. They had been left in ignorance of the petition on which the Bill had been founded. The persons who signed that petition " consisted principally of their ancient oppressors, their noblesse, who wanted nothing more than, as formerly, to domineer over them ; and they exclaimed against them bitterly on that account, but intimated that they had better take care of themselves, and not be too forward to put their intentions into execution."†

After the Bill reached the Province great numbers of the French Canadians offered to join the British colonists in petitioning for the continuance of the English laws. In deference to the wishes of their fellow-citizens of French origin, the committee appointed by the British colonists to prepare petitions to the King, Lords and Commons, for the repeal or amendment of the Act, drew up a petition for the French Canadians to sign. But, at the last moment, the French Canadians stated that " they were withheld by their superiors, and commanded not to join in the English representations ; for if they did they would infallibly be deprived of their religion ; but if they remained quiet, they might depend upon it that the English laws would not be changed." ‡

---

* Maseres, "Additional Papers," p. 101.
† Maseres, "Add. Papers," pp. 102, 103.
‡ Maseres Papers, pp. 133, 134. "Zachary Macaulay" is one name amongst the nine fortifying this statement, which is contained in a letter bearing date "Quebec, Nov. 12, 1774," and is addressed to Baron Maseres. The letter

In opposition to the Quebec Act, the British colonists and the French Canadians did not stand apart from the rest of the empire. The people of the British Islands pronounced against it. For more than two months the newspapers teemed with letters in which the measure was unsparingly criticised and sternly denounced.*

But if the opposition elsewhere were a breeze, the opposition in the Thirteen Colonies was a tempest which shook to its foundations the fabric of British supremacy on this continent. On the 14th of October, 1774, Congress passed a number of resolutions, setting forth their grievances and defining their rights. One resolution declared that during the last session of the British Parliament three statutes were passed. One of them was for " Making more effectual provision for the Government of the Province of Quebec."

All of these statutes were pronounced "impolitic, unjust and cruel, as well as unconstitutional, and most dangerous and destructive of American rights."†

The Quebec Act was described as one " for establishing the Roman Catholic religion in the Province of Quebec, abolishing the equitable system of English laws, and erecting a tyranny there, to the great danger—from its

says further: "In justice to the bulk of the Canadian inhabitants, who have formerly smarted under the rigour of the French Government, and the caprice of petty tyrants of those days, we must confess that they prefer infinitely English law, which secures their liberty and property, and gives a free scope to their industry, and dread falling again under the laws and customs of Canada. This we declare upon our own certain knowledge "

\* Maseres Papers, p. 236.
† American Archives, 4th Series, vol. 1, p. 912.

total dissimilarity to the religion, law and government—of the neighbouring British Colonies, by the assistance of whose blood and treasure the said Colony was conquered from France."*

The Congress, on the 20th of October, 1774, drew up an address to the people of Great Britain, in which address was enumerated a list of grievances. "Several cruel and oppressive Acts have been passed. * * Also an Act for extending the Province of Quebec, so as to border on the western frontiers of these Colonies, establish an arbitrary Government therein, and discourage the settlement of British subjects in that wide-extended country; thus, by the influence of civil principles and ancient prejudices, to dispose the inhabitants to act with hostility against the free Protestant Colonies, whenever a wicked Ministry shall choose so to direct them."†

In the half-alienated Colonies this Quebec Act was as a crushing weight falling from the summit of British power on the straining and weakening bond of kinship‡ which linked the Empire and its offspring. The Bill was framed to retain Canada. It had but faint and fallacious influence in accomplishing that result. But this it did accomplish : it helped to cut adrift from Great

\* Ibid. p. 912.
† Ibid. p. 913.
‡ Baron Maseres, in 1779, said that the Act "had not only offended the inhabitants of the Province (Quebec) itself, in a degree that could hardly be conceived, but had alarmed all the English Provinces in America, and contributed more, perhaps, than any other measure whatsoever to drive them into rebellion against their Sovereign."—Preface to "Debates on Quebec Bill," p. v.

Britain the noblest appendages of sovereignty that ever promised to lend power and splendour to a Parent State. The Mother-land was the loser. We who now behold these things through the calm and settled medium of a century—a medium in which the giants of a hundred years ago are the pigmies of to-day—in which the lines of Providential events are no longer dim and distorted, but clear and straight,—we are forced to ask ourselves and history, if the Empire were the loser, was not Humanity the gainer?

# CHAPTER VI.

DISSATISFACTION OF THE MAJORITY OF THE FRENCH
CANADIANS.—AMERICAN OVERTURES AND INVASION.

THE British Ministry, in the passing of the Quebec Act, had achieved two objects. They had gained over the clergy and the seigniors; and had induced the French Canadian people to recognize the supreme authority of the House of Commons in the matter of taxation.* This race, for generations, was obliged to pay taxes without open murmur or chance of relief. It was unacquainted with the constitutional machinery by which the men of Great Britain could restrain the undue exercise of the taxing power. To the French Canadians, therefore, this power was one they could but too well understand, knowing not how to modify or resist it. For this reason the French Canadians offered no opposition to a Bill which followed the Quebec Act.† The measure was memorable in this—that it was the first tax bill Great Britain ever passed with respect to Canada; and that it abolished the French customs duties, which had been allowed, since the Conquest, to remain unchanged. The preamble recited that certain duties were

---

\* Garneau's "History of Canada," vol. 2, p. 119.
† The title was—"An Act to establish a Fund towards further defraying the charge of the Administration of Justice, and the Support of Civil Government, within the Province of Quebec."

imposed by the authority of His Most Christian Majesty the King of France. These duties were declared to be abolished, and others substituted, after the 5th of April, 1775.*

The composition of the Council was amongst the first grievances of which the French Canadians made complaint. In the year of the passing of the Quebec Act, 1774, Governor Carleton, who had been created a Major-General while in England, returned to Canada, to put the new measure into effect. He appointed a Legislative Council. It numbered twenty-three members; eight of them were Roman Catholics. But the lawyers, notaries, and others, men who had been afraid to refuse their signatures to the petition, almost unanimously declared their dislike to the Act when they saw how the Council was constituted. For a seat had been given to none except to the noblesse or to those who wore the cross of St. Louis. The commercial element amongst the French

---

* The French duties were upon wine, rum, brandy, and *eau de vie de liqueur*, imported into the Province ; also, a duty of three pounds *per centum, ad valorem*, upon all dry goods imported into and exported from the Province. The British duties were—on every gallon of brandy, or other spirits, manufactured in Great Britain, threepence ; on every gallon of rum, or other spirits, imported from any of His Majesty's sugar colonies in the West Indies, sixpence ; on the same articles imported from any other of His Majesty's colonies in America, ninepence ; on every gallon of foreign brandy, or other spirits, foreign manufactured, imported from Great Britain, one shilling ; on every gallon of rum, or spirits, produce or manufacture of American colonies, not British, imported from any other place except Great Britain, one shilling ; on every gallon of molasses, or syrups, imported into Canada in British, Irish, and Canadian vessels, threepence ; on the same articles imported into Canada in foreign vessels, sixpence. [It will be seen that vessels belonging to the Thirteen Colonies are not included.]

Canadians had not a single representative in the Council.*

In the latter part of the year 1774, the Americans, feeling that their hour of trial was at hand, and their raw and immature power about to engage in deadly grapple with the strength of a firm and time-tried Empire, began to turn their eyes Canada-ward. From the Canadians, their enemies for generations, they sought aid and comfort in the rapidly nearing struggle with the mother country. In the " Address of the General Congress to the Inhabitants of the Province of Quebec," dated October 26th, 1774, and signed by Henry Middleton, President, the theory of Constitutional Government was developed at considerable length. Then there was pointed out the instances in which this theory was violated by the Quebec Act. The address concluded thus—" In this present Congress * * it has been with universal pleasure, and a unanimous vote, resolved—That we should consider the violation of your rights, by the Act for altering the government of your Province, as a violation of our own ; and that you should be invited to accede to our Confederation, which has no other objects than the perfect security of the natural and civil rights of all the constituent members, according to their respective circumstances, and the preservation of a happy and lasting connection with Great Britain, on the salutary and constitutional principles hereinbefore mentioned." On the 1st day of May,

* Maseres, Add. Papers, p. 102.

1775, the Quebec Act went into effect. On the 29th of the same month, the American Congress addressed the Canadians: "We most sincerely condole with you on the arrival of that day, in the course of which the sun could not shine on a single freeman, in all your extensive dominions. By the introduction of your present form of government, or rather present form of tyranny, you and your wives and your children are made slaves."*

The address was not barren of serious results. Translated into the French language, it was sent for distribution to Messrs. Walker and Cazeau, influential British and French merchant of Montreal, who made no secret of having received it. The address had reached Canada through American newspapers. It had also been handed about the country by the French Canadians themselves.†

The peasants in the rural districts felt its influence. Not a few of the British colonists in the towns were swayed by the constitutional sympathies to which it gave expression.‡ In all great popular movements a wave of

* Bancroft, vol. 7, pp. 381, 382. He adds—"No adequate motive for rising was set before them. * * A union for independence, with a promise of institutions of their own, might have awakened their enthusiasm."

† Maseres, Add. Pap. p. 85. For over the century and a half—1608-1760— during which France ruled Canada, a printing press never entered the country. In 1764, an English newspaper, the *Quebec Gazette*, was established. This pioneer of the grand array of journals that now do duty for Canada, its liberties and its colonial pre-eminence, still flourishes.

‡ See Bancroft, vol. 8, p. 177. "The French nobility, of whom many, under the Quebec Act, were received into the Council or appointed to Executive offices, and the Catholic clergy who were restored to the possession of their estates and their tithes, acquiesced in the new form of government, but by a large part of the British residents it was detested, as at war with English liberties, and subjecting them to arbitrary power. The instincts of the Canadian pea-

human feeling goes out, which overflows the barriers of place, race and faith, and, with a mysterious influence, sucks into the whirl and vortex of the struggle every one who, having a grievance that bows him down, stands hoping on the marge of the Future, holding out his hands to welcome a coming change. In such case was the majority of the French Canadians and British colonists of Canada, in relation to the approaching strife between England and her colonies. On the 19th of April, 1775, at Lexington, blood had flowed out upon the quarrel ; had burned hatred into the hearts of the opposing kinsmen, and set two continents on fire. It is not within the scope and purport of this work to narrate the incidents of this most lamentable war, except in so far as those incidents may relate to the social and political condition of Canada.

On the 1st of June, 1775, Congress passed a resolution : "That, as this Congress has nothing more in view than the defence of these colonies, no expedition or incursion ought to be undertaken or made by any colony, or body of colonists, against or into Canada."* The resolution was translated into French, and distributed throughout Canada. In the light of the subsequent action of Congress, this resolution must be regarded as an attempt to cheat either the Government or people of Canada into a

santry inclined them to take part with the United Colonies ; they denied the authority of the French nobility as magistrates, and resisted their claim of a right as seigniors to command their military services. Without the hardihood to rise of themselves, they were willing to welcome invasion."

* Lord Mahon's " History of England," vol. 6, p. 92.

sense of security, the better to overrun and overwhelm them. For, on the 27th of June Congress passed another resolution, instructing General Schuyler to proceed without delay to Ticonderoga, and, if he found it practicable, "immediately to take possession of St. John's and Montreal, and pursue any other measure in Canada which might have a tendency to promote the peace and security of these Colonies."*

These things did not escape the notice of Governor Carleton, one of the most praiseworthy military men that ever governed a British dependency ; the man who preserved Canada to the Empire ; the only English General who extorted from the Americans an honourable reputation for generosity and humanity.† Carleton, on the 9th of June, 1775, proclaimed that he had put the Province under martial law ; at the same time he called out its militia. The malign influence of the Quebec Act, now that the fate of Canada was about to be placed in the balance of war, was everywhere felt in disastrous dis-

* Lord Mahon's "Hist. Eng.," vol. 6, pp. 114, 115. In a note on this resolution, Lord Mahon remarks—"This last resolution being kept secret or not printed in the journals, it is a hard task to vindicate, on this occasion, either the good faith or the consistency of the American rulers." The last observation might, with safety, be applied to almost every case, from 1775 to 1873, in which the rights of Canada came into conflict with the interests of the United States. The Maine and Oregon Boundaries, and the Island of San Juan, rise up in accusation against the United States' contempt of the higher law of International Equity. Bancroft's defence of the action of Congress is, that on the 9th of June Governor Carleton "proclaimed the American borderers to be a rebellious band of traitors, established martial law," etc. (See vol. 8, p. 176.) Most unprejudiced minds will refuse to see in this defence a successful exoneration of the double-dealing of Congress.

† Bancroft, vol. 8, p. 186.

appointment. Now was seen by the perplexed Governor of Canada, the fatuous folly of the measure that gave bread, power and privilege to a church and a noblesse, and to the people stones and serpents. The noblesse were hated; the clergy were powerless, if not absolutely despised; and the bosom of the Province was left open to the blows of the American invader.

# CHAPTER VII.

ANTAGONISM OF SEIGNIOR AND PEASANT.—THE PEASANTS REFUSE MILITARY SERVICE TO THE SEIGNIORS.

THE peasants believed that the Quebec Act revived those powers of Crown and noble which had been their scourge and their horror in the French period.* An opinion prevailed in the Province, that the seigniors, by the tenure of their lands, owed military service to the King of England. Further, that it was part of the same tenure, that they should engage for the personal service of all their vassals. It was also believed that, as the Quebec Act revived the laws and customs of Canada, the seigniors had a legal right, whenever the King or his representative called on them, to command the personal service of all their tenants.†

It was soon seen that the times were changed. In the fourteen years of British rule, the French Canadian peasant had made brave progress up the ascent of personal liberty, whence he stood and gazed back in fear across the slough of servitude over which his ancestors had toiled and panted for over a century and a half. The seignior of Terrebonne, M. La Corne, was deputed by General Carleton to enrol his tenants. La Corne took high ground

* Maseres, Add. Pap. p. 69.
† Maseres, Add. Pap. pp. 71, 72.

with the peasants. He told them that, by the tenure of their lands, he had a right to command their military services. Their answer was the most pregnant commentary on the Conquest: "They were now become subjects of England, and did not look on themselves as Frenchmen in any respect whatever."* Then followed uproar.† A Mr. Deschambaud, son of a seignior, went to his father's estate on the River Richelieu, to raise the tenants. He harangued them in an arbitrary strain. They replied defiantly. He then drew his sword; whereupon the people surrounded him, and beat him severely. The result of this incident might have been fraught with the very worst consequences, had it not been for the admirable tact of Carleton.‡ Mr. Cuthbert, an Englishman, seignior of Berthier, made a peremptory demand on the military service of his tenants. They told him not a man of them would follow him; and made an oath on the public cross, at the place of meeting, that they would never take

---

* Maseres, Add. Pap. p. 73.

† M. La Corne struck some of those who spoke loudest; this maddened the people. He was forced to fly to Montreal, threatening to bring back two hundred soldiers. The people armed themselves for resistance, determined to die rather than submit to the seignior. But the prudence of Carleton soothed them. He would not give La Corne soldiers; but sent with him an English officer, a Capt. Hamilton. In reply to Hamilton the people said: "If Gen. Carleton requires our services, let him give us English officers to command us; * * or if not, common soldiers, rather than those people" (the seigniors). The peasants only dispersed when Hamilton promised that La Corne should come no more among them.—Maseres, Add. Pap. p. 74.

‡ The peasants, fearing that it might go ill with them, assembled to the number of three thousand at Fort Chambly, and began to march to Fort St. John's, to face two regiments of regulars there, whom they suspected the Governor would use against them. Carleton promised to forgive them if they dispersed; they did so, and he kept his word.—Maseres, Add. Pap. p. 76.

up arms against the Americans; that if any one of them
offered to join the Government, they would burn his
house and barn, and destroy his cattle; and that, if Carleton attempted to compel them into the service, they would
repel force by force.* M. Lanaudiere, seignior of St.
Anne's, went to Berthier to make the attempt in which
Cuthbert failed. The people seized him, with seventeen
of his companions, and held warm debates as to whether
they should send him to the American camp at St. John's.
Finally, on his promise to obtain for them the Governor's
pardon, and never again to come amongst them on a like
errand, he and his friends were set at liberty.†

The main reason why the peasants—when aroused, a
determined and warlike race—refused to do military service was, not that they disliked their new rulers, but that
they detested the new Bill. The men of Berthier declared
that if Governor Carleton would promise, and affix the
promise to the church door, that he would do his best for
the repeal of the Quebec Bill, they were ready to defend
the Province. They said "that on a sudden, without
any provocation on their part, they had been reduced to
their former state of slavery. They were told to regard
the invaders as enemies. But then the invaders said
that they were not enemies, but their best friends. The
invaders were now in arms for the defence of the peasants
from their oppressors; and made the repeal of the Quebec
Bill one of the conditions for laying down their arms.

* Mascres, Add. Pap. pp. 76, 77.
† Masoros, Add. Pap. 77, 78.

56   CONSTITUTIONAL HISTORY OF CANADA.

The peasants, then, ought certainly to assist those who were fighting to restore to them that liberty of which they had been wantonly and most cruelly deprived." This language, however, was not that of the men of Berthier alone. "The same is in the mouths of the most ignorant peasants all over the Province."*

But it was not the peasants only to whom the Quebec Act was a menace and a grievance. The men of the towns held the measure in detestation. In Montreal, the captain of the French Canadian Militia declared to Carleton "that his compatriots would not take arms as a militia unless His Excellency would assure them, on his honour, that he would use his utmost endeavours to get the Quebec Bill repealed." The Governor thereupon gave the promise.†

The Government of Canada felt that it had, in all justice and generosity, an irresistible claim on the Roman Catholic Church in the Province. It invoked the aid of the Church to influence the peasants. But the children closed their ears against the advice of their Mother, and steeled their hearts against her entreaties.

---

* Maseres, Add. Pap. pp. 78, 79. The conduct of the peasants drew out hints from the Government, that their refusal to obey the seigniors had justified the forfeiture of their lands, and that suits at law would be taken to dispossess them. The peasants admitted that they had incurred forfeiture, but were determined to hold possession of their lands by force.—Maseres, Add. Pap. p. 72. Happily for Canada and Great Britain, the soldier-statesman who governed the Province did not allow any actions for forfeiture to be taken.

† Maseres, Add. Pap. p. 106.

# CHAPTER VIII.

THE STATUS OF THE ROMAN CATHOLIC CHURCH.—THE
PEASANTS REFUSE IT POLITICAL OBEDIENCE.

INASMUCH as before the Conquest, since that epoch, and at the present time, the Roman Catholic Church in Lower Canada must be regarded as one of the chief elements in the social and political life of that Province, it becomes necessary to devote a portion of space to a sketch of the fortunes of the establishment. After the Conquest, the Grand Vicar and Clergy of Quebec, the see being vacant by the death of its former occupant, Mgr. Pontbriant, applied to the Governor, General Murray, asking that their right to elect should be recognised. The Governor transmitted the matter to the Home authorities, and recommended the granting of the demand. In 1763 the Law Officers of the Crown decided that the Penal Laws against the Roman Catholics in the British Islands did not extend to the Colonies. Accordingly, the Chapter of Quebec elected as their Bishop, M. de Montgolfier, Superior of the Seminary of St. Sulpice, Montreal. The Government took exception to the nomination.\* M. de Montgolfier, in 1764, declined the charge. At the same time he designated M. Briand, a Breton by birth,

\* " Perhaps because the nominee was too French at heart."—Garneau," Hist. Can.," vol. 2, p. 89.

one of the Canons and Grand Vicar of Quebec, for the vacant Episcopate. M. Briand was chosen. In the same year, 1764, he visited London, and received, with the consent of the King, his bulls of investiture from Pope Clement XIII. ; and then repairing to Paris, was there consecrated. To the Province of Quebec, which had been without a Bishop from 1760 to 1766, Mgr. Briand returned in the latter year, a stipendiary of the King of England to the extent of £200 sterling annually.* His acceptance of the yearly pension, and his subsequent administration, contributed to his unpopularity and lessened his influence.† It seemed, on his return to Canada, that he would exercise only the milder and more beneficent duties of his high office. In his reply to those who welcomed his arrival he deprecated pomp and ceremony. He told them that "he did not come into the Province to be a Bishop on the same high footing as his predecessors in the time of the French Government : * * * that he was *un simple faiseur de prêtres*—a mere ordainer of priests."‡ But power ultimately became too strong for sobriety of ecclesiastical demeanour.§ The Bishop, in a manner unknown to Canadian ecclesiastical history, before or since, launched forward on a career of pre-

* Maseres, Add. Pap. p. 137.  Bancroft, vol. 8, p. 177, alludes to Bishop Briand as "a stipendiary of the British King."
† Maseres, Add. Pap. p. 137.
‡ *Ibid*, 138.
§ See "Anecdotes sur la conduite de Monsieur Briand, Evêque de Québec. Extrait d'une lettre de Québec de la fin de Septembre, 1775, à un ami à Londres. Maseres, Add. Pap. pp. 120–126.

rogative. He suspended and deprived priests; he cut off members of his faith from their sacraments; he interdicted divine worship in churches and chapels.* The Bishop may have resorted to these measures in his loyalty to the British Government. But in any community, whether made up of one or of many faiths, no matter whether a Government or the people are the first to begin dispute, ecclesiastical aid, come from whatever creed it may, is a dangerous and exacting auxiliary. The defeated party perpetuates the quarrel by the bitter hatred which they are sure to cherish against their spiritual antagonists. For the natural instincts of men tell them that the glory of the Christian faith is to make peace, to mediate, to fly from strife as from a plague. The politician who wields a spiritual weapon makes wounds that centuries will not heal; nor can he return the sword to the scabbard until its owners have secured for the use of it powers and privileges which, in unscrupulous hands, may, in her time of need, coerce and confront the very majesty of the State which surrendered them.

Mgr. Briand, Roman Catholic Bishop of Quebec, issued in the summer of 1775, at the instance of the Government, an encyclical letter to the French Canadian people. In this epistle the Bishop exhorted them to take up arms for the Crown against the American invaders. To those who obeyed, he promised indulgences. Over the heads of those who should refuse, he suspended the thunders of

* Maseres, Add. Pap. pp. 138, 139.

excommunication. The reception accorded to the letter was another instance of a phenomenon sometimes witnessed in history—that when the political passions of men begin to boil, the elements of religious kinship and obligation begin to evaporate. The very quarrel then in progress between Great Britain and her colonies was proof to the point.

The people not only turned deaf ears to the injunctions of the Bishop, but expressed the opinion that his action in the dispute was quite unsuitable to the character of a Christian prelate, who ought to have no concern in anything that involved the shedding of blood. They even went further than this. They assumed that Bishop Briand's conduct had been influenced by the pension of £200 a year he received from the King of England, and by the expectation he had formed of a larger gratuity.* The French Canadians not only disobeyed their Bishop, but went so far as to lampoon him in more than thirty songs, which were circulated during the summer of 1775.† Fifty placards, affixed to public places, testified to the sentiments which the prelate had excited in his people. "He had been issuing forth throughout every part of the Province one excommunication after another. It was no longer the King who was disobeyed, but the Church, of which the Bishop was the head. His

---

* Maseres, Add. Pap. p. 112. (Bishop Briand was probably the first Roman Catholic Bishop, since the time of Queen Mary, who received an annual stipend from a British monarch.)

† Maseres, Add. Pap. pp. 117, 118.

violent conduct, which only exasperated the people," had lasted from the 20th of May until the early part of November (1775), when he became quiet, " even threatening to leave the Province and go to France." A devout wish was expressed that he would carry out the threat. "But it was only the fear of the Americans, who had invaded the country, which had caused him to make it."‡ In one of the lampoons the people were made, in sarcasm, to say to themselves—" In disregard of true glory, they ought to march forward, though they would earn but a sorry niche in the Temple of Memory. However, by their heroic deeds in battle, they would deserve this —that the pension of the Bishop should be largely augmented."§

‡ The above facts are contained in a French letter in the " Maseres' Add. Papers," pp. 117-18. It is in part as follows:—"On dit que plus de 30 chansons et 50 placards, où la cupidité * * * Il (the Bishop) envoye, en haut et en bas du païs excommunications sur excommunications. Ce n'est plus au roi qu'on desobèit ; c'est à l'église, dont il est le chef. Sa folie (qui ne fait qu'irriter les peuples), dure depuis le 20 de May. Cependant depuis le 3me de ce mois (Novembre) il se tait :—menace même le païs de s'en aller en France. Plût à Dieu qu' il exécutât sa menace ! Mais ce n'est que la peur qu'il a des Bostonnois qui la lui fait faire."

§ The first eight verses of the song it would be offensive to reproduce. The words of the last two verses, 9 and 10, were :—

" En dépit de la vraie gloire
   Partons nos pas en avant.
   Dans le Temple de Mémoire
   Nous serons mis tristement.

   Et, par nos braves prouesses
   Dans les combats, méritons
   Qu'on augmente avec largesse
   Du prélat la pension."

Maseres, Add. Pap. pp. 112, 113, 114.

# CHAPTER IX.

PERIL OF THE PROVINCE.—AMERICAN ATTACK ON QUEBEC.—DEFEAT AND EXPULSION OF THE INVADERS.

THE situation of the Province was one of extreme peril. The position of Governor Carleton was that of a ruler weighed down by perplexity, and rendered powerless by being deserted by those on whom he had relied. Turn to whatever quarter he might, he saw no chance of being enabled to cope successfully with the invaders. In the month of October, 1775, he succeeded in assembling 900 men at Montreal, to operate against the Americans who were engaged in besieging one or two wretched places on the Eastern Frontier, before they marched on that city. But the force melted away. The French Canadians, in the same month, actually turned the scale for the invaders in capturing the Fort of Chambly.* The Governor, with 800 Indians, French Canadians and regulars he had enrolled "with desperate exertions," endeavoured to effect a junction with Col. Maclean, in order to raise the siege of St. Johns. Carleton met with a reverse ; then the French Canadians deserted Maclean. † St. Johns, on Nov. the 3rd, after a gallant defence of 50 days, surrendered to the Americans. Its garrison, 500

* Bancroft, vol. 8, p. 186.
† Bancroft, vol. 8, p. 187.

CONSTITUTIONAL HISTORY OF CANADA. 63

regulars and 100 French Canadians, many of whom were of the seigniorial class, marched out with the honours of war.*

The road to Montreal was now open. In the matter of apathy in the defence of the country, and as far as regarded sympathy with the invaders, a portion of the British colonists were of the same frame of mind as the majority of the French Canadians. If blame is to be awarded, some of the British colonists must bear their share. Neither race can be much praised at the expense of the other. It ought to be remarked, however, that several English gentlemen in Montreal, men of experience in military matters, offered their services to lead the Canadians. But, for some unaccountable reason, the Governor refused them. †

General Montgomery, on the 12th of November, 1775, took unopposed possession of the City of Montreal.‡ The Thirteen Colonies were now masters of all Canada,

* Ibid. vol. 8, p. 188.
† Maseres, Add. Papers, p. 79. In page 80 it is stated "that the English inhabitants, though they felt for their treatment from Governor Carleton, yet did not think it would justify their countenancing, in any degree, those who were in arms against their sovereign. Accordingly they have been active in the defence of the Province; those few Canadians who have taken part with the Government have been influenced entirely by their persuasion and example."
‡ Governor Carleton, utterly powerless, was obliged, on the eve of the entrance of the invaders into Montreal, to leave the city by stealth, and, accompanied by a handful of men, to try to reach Quebec by the St. Lawrence, eluding the guard boats of the Americans, stationed at various points along the river. Part of the way he had to disguise himself as a peasant. After many hair-breadth escapes from capture, fortunately for British rule in Canada, he reached Quebec on the 17th November.

with the exception of the City of Quebec. This, the key of the Province, was still held by the smitten but firm-closed hand of Great Britain. *  On the last day of the old year, 1775, in the ghastly light of a winter dawn, the raw and marrow-piercing air choked with the rush of stinging snow-flakes, an icy acclivity beneath his feet, a mountain fortress above his head, death staring him in front, and despondency threatening him behind, General Richard Montgomery rushed forward to the supreme struggle with Great Britain for her Canadian Empire. He failed and fell. † The Province was saved. Carleton, an enemy no less generous than Montgomery himself, gave to the clay of his old comrade in arms under Wolfe, the honours of a soldier's sepulture. In a few months more Canada expelled from her violated soil the last American invader.

The moral of this eventful year is easy to understand. The politicians, not the statesmen of Great Britain, after having lashed the Thirteen Colonies into revolt, fancied they might oppose to the Democratic wave, now in angry and vehement flow, the cobweb barrier of class legislation. The act was akin to that of the Persian

* " On Dec. the 22nd, Carleton ordered all who would not join in the defence of the city, to leave it within four days. After their departure he found himself supported by more than 300 regulars, 330 Anglo-Canadian militia, 543 French Canadians, 485 seamen and marines, 120 artificers capable of bearing arms." In all 1,778 men. " On the 5th December, the invading army was composed of less than 1,000 American troops, and a volunteer regiment of about 200 Canadians."—Bancroft, vol. 8, pp. 200, 201. As Canadians, we can afford to say that the advantages were on the side of our own countrymen.

†Bancroft, vol. 8, p. 208, says, that, with Montgomery, "the soul of the expedition fled."

despot scourging the rebellious billows of the Hellespont, which mocked him still the more with their defiant thunders. The Quebec Bill spurned the rights of the people of Canada; it raised thrones for prelates and aristocrats. In the day of danger the prelates were weak, and the aristocrats were as stubble. But it was many a sorrowful year ere British Ministers would learn or acknowledge that if they unshackled the arms of the men of Canada, these men would know how to hold for Great Britain, as against all who would attempt to seize it, the sovereignty of the North American Empire.

# CHAPTER X.

COLONIAL MISGOVERNMENT.—FRENCH CANADIAN LEGISLATIVE COUNCILLORS OPPOSE HABEAS CORPUS.

In the history of Great Britain and her Colonies, many have been the instances in which the latter have experienced refusals when they looked for concessions. Now, when the Colonies march step for step with the Mother Land on the road which leads to a future of brighter social and political life, the offspring of Great Britain, separated from her by oceans never so wide, can judge of her past acts, not with feelings of bitterness, but with feelings of leniency and allowance.

It is plain to the student of our colonial history, that in almost every case, in times past, in which the relations between Great Britain and Canada were those of authority rather than affection, the fault, as a rule, lay not so much at the door of the British Ministers of the day, as to the charge of those who occupied high places of trust in our Provincial Administrations. There is little doubt that British Ministers made effort to do their best, or what they thought was best. There is less doubt that the Provincial officers in whom they trusted for a full and accurate recital of those social facts and popular aspirations without which legislation is as brick without straw, were recreant to the confidence which had been reposed in them. The British Minister felt himself bound to believe the information transmitted to him by the Governor. The Governor received his information from the members of a colonial oligarchy, who stood like an impassable rampart between the people and the representative of Great Britain. No sounds but the scented echo of artificial praise, and the grateful breezes of fictitious popular delight, were ever permitted to steal upon the ear of the British Governor. The people's discontent might sweep over the land in gusts whose force and frequency were the forerunners of a terrible tempest, but the Governors were never allowed to hear the mutterings without. In the official atmosphere everything was bathed in brightness, and all was repose. To change a figure in the simile of the Roman poet, doomed to be the flatterer of a Court, not the celebrant of a free people, the Canadian Governor, surrounded by that mockery of feudalism, a Canadian oligarchy, shone above them in the treacherously peaceful firmament of the official universe, while they rejoiced in being the smaller stars.*

In the matter of the unfortunate Quebec Bill, there can be no doubt that it was founded upon partial information. Ministers, it is to be assumed in charity, endeavoured to do what they considered right and just. But they acted in ignorance of the needs and wishes of the majority of the people of both races. And to attempt to do right in ignorance is almost as mischievous as

\* "Nox erat, et luna in cælo sereno fulgebat,
Inter minora sidera."—*Horace.*

to do wrong with full knowledge. For their ignorance the advisers of the Crown were only partially to blame. The burden of the blame must rest with their Canadian officials. To give the British Ministry justice, they showed signs of being desirous to mitigate some of the more oppressive results which flowed from the Quebec Bill. They had evidently been moved by the petitions of the British colonists, and were prepared to make concessions. The facts now about to be related have been kept from the knowledge of the people of Canada. But the time has come to let the light of 'truth shine in upon the dark places of our history, and to apply the caustic of criticism to the unwholesome growths of national pretence and self-adulation.

' The Quebec Bill had not long become law when the Earl of Dartmouth, Secretary of State for America, directed Mr. Hey, Chief Justice of the Province of Quebec, to prepare the draft of a Provincial ordinance. This, the Chief Justice was to carry over to Canada, in order to lay it before the Governor and the new Legislative Council, so that they might make it into a law. The draft provided for the re-establishment of the English laws relating to *habeas corpus;* to commerce; and, with certain restrictions, to trial by jury in civil cases. In the month of September, 1775, the draft was submitted to the Legislative Council of Canada and made the subject of debate. The new French-Canadian members opposed it, " but without (as it is said) alleging any reasons for their opposition."* The British members of the Council seemed disposed to adopt the ordinance. It would probably have become law, but for the fact that General Montgomery's invasion compelled Governor Carleton to break up the meetings of the Council before the discussion of the subject came to a conclusion. In this instance was shown what, in the after history of the country, was the bitter experience of its inhabitants, that a non-elective Legislative Body was the natural enemy of popular liberty. The opposition made by the French-Canadian members to the re-establishment of trial by jury and the English commercial code, was nothing but what might have been expected. Their antagonism to the revival of *habeas corpus* was, as they well knew, in direct hostility to the earnest wishes of the British colonists, as also to the desires of the great majority of the French. But the chevaliers of the Cross of St. Louis did after their kind. Unfortunately for many a Canadian, French and British, the action of these seigniors, in baffling the wishes of the people for security for personal liberty, was destined to work wide evil and bitter suffering in the days that were about to come.

* The words within commas are those of the document on which the above statement is based.—Maseres, Add. Pap., pp. 447, 448.

# CHAPTER XI.

REVIVAL OF THE FRENCH LAWS.—NATURE OF THESE LAWS.

National prepossession should never be allowed to suppress truth or to cloak fact. And it is both truth and fact to say that the administration of justice was the one bright and laudable characteristic of the French rule in Canada.

The Great Ordinance of the 17th of September, 1764, introduced at once into Canada all the civil and criminal laws of England. In the wording of the Ordinance it was assumed that, " in the Supreme Court sitting at Quebec, his Britannic Majesty was present in the person of his Chief Justice, having full power to determine all civil and criminal cases, agreeably to the laws of England and to the ordinances of this Province." But there were British legists, even in those days, who contended, with the weapons of constitutional precedent, that this "sudden and violent act of legislation" was void and illegal, and that, of right, the French laws should have remained in force in Canada.* The arguments may be thus stated :—
The change of laws had not been made by the Parliament of Great Britain, which was the only proper Legislature

* For an able argument on this subject see pp. 35–47 of a paper in the first vol. of the " Lower Canada Jurist," entitled " A View of the Civil Government and Administration of Justice in the Province of Canada, while it was subject to the Crown of France."

CONSTITUTIONAL HISTORY OF CANADA. 71

of Canada. The change had not been made by virtue of any legislative authority legally communicated by the King to the Governor and Council of Canada. For the commission, under the great seal to the Governor, communicated no such authority to the Governor and Council, but to the Governor, Council and Assembly. The King's private instructions were not a legal method of communicating such an authority. Further, the change had been made without a promulgation of the new laws.

/ The supplanted law of Canada was a body of jurisprudence known as the " Custom of Paris." The Province was divided into three judicial districts, each of which took its name from its principal town—Quebec, Three Rivers and Montreal. In each of these districts a judge, appointed by the King, had full jurisdiction in all cases, criminal and civil. These judges sat twice a week throughout the year. The exceptions were about six weeks of vacation in September and October, and a fortnight at Easter. If litigants so desired it, the judges, upon being allowed a certain moderate allowance for their extra labour, would sit oftener than once a week. In Quebec and Montreal each judge had an assistant, to take his place in case of sickness or absence. The judges had no option in the modification of the laws, but from all decisions there lay an appeal to the Supreme Council. From the Supreme Council there lay a further appeal to the King of France himself, in his Council of State.

The Supreme Council, numbering fifteen members, was

composed of the principal officials of the civil government, and of men of eminence in the Province. The Governor, the Intendant and the Bishop of Quebec were of the Council; they had a right to sit and vote, but seldom attended. The Council was solely a Court of Appeal for all matters civil and criminal; no suit could be originally instituted in it. The Council could relax penalties in criminal and civil offences, and often exercised this power. It sat once a week throughout the year, except in the Autumn vacation and during the Easter solemnities. At the urgent demand of suitors the Court would sit oftener than once a week.

To each of the jurisdictions of Quebec, Three Rivers and Montreal, there was attached a "Procureur du Roi," or Attorney for the King. In this officer was vested the power of a Grand Jury; it was his duty to inform the Court of the commission of a crime, and to indict the offender. The mode of procedure of the Attorney was very cautious. A person who knew of the commission of a crime called on him voluntarily, was examined, and the evidence taken down in writing. If the Attorney suspected that others besides the voluntary witness knew anything of the crime, such persons he had a right to summon and examine. The witnesses were always questioned separately. If, after the private examinations, the officer considered that he ought to proceed further by way of public trial, he prayed the Court for power of arrest. But if the Attorney thought that the private examinations were not of such a nature as to warrant a prosecution, the person privately accused was never molested. If this officer allowed, in his district, an offence to pass unexamined, he was held guilty of a misdemeanor. It was also the duty of the Attorney to sue for the King's civil rights : such as taxes, fines upon the alienation of land, escheats of lands on the commission of certain great crimes, or the breach of the conditions of tenure. He was obliged, as well, to sue for the rights of all persons and corporations that were under the protection of the Crown : such as orphans, absentees and churches. Further, it was his duty to cause the King's Ordinances, and those of the Supreme Council, to be entered in the Court Registers of his district, and to be duly published.

There was an officer known as the King's Attorney-General. His duty was to transact the King's business in the Supreme Council or Court of Appeal, and to supervise the three Attorneys.

Such were the King's regular law courts. But there was another court of a peculiar jurisdiction : this was the Court of the Intendant. It had power to determine civil matters in a summary manner. The jurisdiction was seldom exercised except in such causes as would not bear the cost of litigation in the King's Courts. The people found the Intendant's Court of great advantage, and frequently sought its interference. The Intendant had deputies; their jurisdiction, but not his, was limited to suits not exceeding fifty French livres, or about forty shillings sterling.

E

# CHAPTER XII.

LAWS OF INHERITANCE.—DETESTATION OF PRIMOGENITURE.

It was the abolition of their own system of civil laws, and the substitution of that of England, which weighed the most heavily on the French Canadians. In almost every aspect the two legal systems, British and French, were antagonistic. The unnatural custom of primogeniture had no place in the laws of Canada, nor in the hearts of its people.* In respect to the law of inheritance amongst the seigniors, the custom was not to give all to the eldest son. In every case where there were more than two children, the eldest son received only the half of the estate. If there were only two children—that is to say, the eldest son and another—the two-thirds of the estate went to the eldest. As to the law of inheritance in the lands of the peasants, all the children received an equal portion. A restraint, however, was imposed in the case of both seignior and peasant, in order to prevent the evils that might flow from too minute subdivision amongst the co-heirs of the last possessor. If the eldest son of the eldest branch of the original seignior's family had no more of the seigniory remaining to him than the manor-house, and the ground close adjoining it and be-

* The British colonists were willing to have the law of primogeniture expressly excluded, and the French law on that subject expressly revived.— Maseres, Add. Pap. pp. 323, 324.

longing to it—called the *vol du chapon*, or capon's range—subdivision ceased. If such an eldest son had a dozen children, his eldest would inherit the whole of this remnant of the seigniory. In the peasant's case, it was a law that no one should settle and build upon a less quantity of land than sixty superficial *arpents*, or about fifty English acres. A peasant who possessed such a piece of land, dying and leaving several children, it was not divided amongst them, but was to be sold, and the price was to be equally divided amongst all the children. If the elder brother were able, it was usual for him to buy out the rights of the others. If he were unable to do this, it was optional with the second, third or fourth brother to purchase. It was only when any one of all the brothers was unable or unwilling to satisfy the rights of the rest, that the land was sold out of the family.

The character of the criminal and civil jurisprudence of French Canada has now been fairly and fully delineated. It was a code well suited to the genius of the people, for it was the natural outcome of their social life and their political institutions. The great defect of the system was, that it was not strong enough to interpose itself between the people and the tyranny of King and noble. This shortcoming, however, may be fairly charged to the timidity and the time-serving of the Parliaments of Old France, rather than to the inherent fault of the jurisprudence itself. To abolish, in particular, the French civil code was the greatest grievance of the Conquest.

The British civil code was not better for French Canada than the one it had supplanted. The man would justly win the crown of folly who would pretend that every custom and ordinance of England is good for every race, under all circumstances. The French civil laws were best for Canada a century ago. Recast, a few years since, the same laws now regulate the civil interests of the Province of Quebec. The re-establishment of these laws was an équitable concession made to the French Canadians by the Quebec Act of 1774.

# CHAPTER XIII.

#### FEUDAL TENURE: PEASANT SERVITUDES.

The title of "Seignior" meant, in Canada, the lord and owner of an estate which he held directly from the King of France, "en fief or en roture."* The tracts of land thus granted to the seigniors were seldom less than six English miles square, and were often more.† If the seigniory were sold, the purchaser was obliged to pay to the King what was known as the "quint," or a fifth part of the whole purchase money. One of the conditions on which the King granted the lands was, that the seigniors, as soon as possible, should cause them to be settled. For this purpose the seigniors were compelled to make grants of lands to those who applied for them. The grantees and their heirs were entitled to hold their lands for ever, under the grantor and his heirs.

Tenure in "franc aleu" was a freehold tenure; lands so held were exempt from all seigniorial rights and dues, the occupants acknowledging the King alone. But there were in all the Province only two fiefs so held.‡ Lands

---

* "*Fief*," in feudal law, meant an estate in land held of a superior under the charge of fealty, homage and military service. "*Roture*" meant, in old French and Canadian law, a free tenure without the privilege of nobility.

† The Seigniory of Lauzon, near Quebec, on the opposite side of the St. Lawrence, usually known as the Seigniory of Point Levis, and which belonged to General Murray, was eighteen miles square, and contained 324 square miles.

‡ These were Charlesbourg, near Quebec; and 600 "arpents" near Three Rivers, held by the Jesuits.

were occasionally held by "bail emphitéotique," which was equivalent to a long lease of fifty or more years, the lease carrying a small annual rent. There was also a feudal tenure known as the censive; it created a moderate annual rent, paid in money or produce.

The peasant tenure was charged with many oppressive burdens. If the peasant sold his land, the buyer, after paying its price to the seller, was obliged to give to the seignior, over and above that price, the twelfth part of the amount of the purchase money. This seigniorial right was known as "lods et ventes." In case of the prompt payment of the "lods et ventes," it was usual to reduce them by a fourth. The seignior, in the matter of a sale, possessed the "droit de retrait." This was the privilege of pre-emption, within forty days after the sale, at the highest price that had been obtained. This right, however, was not often exercised. The seignior received a tithe of all the fish caught within his domain, or an equivalent sum. It was his right to fell timber anywhere within his seigniory, for the purpose of erecting mills, repairing roads or making new ones. The peasant was compelled to grind his grain at the "moulin banal," or his lord's mill; one-fourteenth part was taken as payment. He was also obliged to perform "corvee," or enforced labour, on the highways and byways. For his rent, he paid every year to the seignior between two shillings and sixpence and five shillings for every "arpent" which his farm extended in front. To this was added some article of food, as a bushel of wheat. From the fines paid in the seigniorial courts, by persons convicted of petty offences, the seigniors derived, in addition to their other revenues, some pecuniary advantages. In their own courts, also, the seigniors sued their tenants for the quit rents and other dues. In the case of tenants who died without heirs, and intestate, the seignior was entitled to the escheat of their lands and goods. If this right, however, were not conferred in the seignior's original grant of jurisdiction, the escheats reverted to the King. The peasants could not make grants of their lands to be holden of themselves. They were obliged to sell outright, and the buyer took the seller's place, and assumed his feudal obligations in respect to the seignior.

The one redeeming feature in the seigniorial system was this, that the peasant was, in spite of the feudal obligations, the absolute owner of his farm. His lord could not dispossess him ; nor, after the fashion of the majority of the Irish and Highland Scotch landlords, drive him and his wife and little ones out to die on the highways and in the ditches, of cold and hunger. The French Canadian peasant was, with his lord, a co-proprietor of the soil. In comparison with the tenant-serfs of Ireland and the Scottish Highlands, the French Canadian farmer was independent. From the land which his fathers and himself had reclaimed and made valuable, he could not be barbarously uprooted by his lord. The Canadian seignior was a man of a more equitable type than the average Irish and Highland landlord. He was also of the same race and faith as his nominal tenant.

But even if he were all these, the State did not leave him to himself, for it threw its shield between him and the peasant. Much of the happiness and prosperity of our country is owing to the fact that we have never been, and never will be, cursed with a land system which, until the humane and far-sighted statesman who now wields the destinies of Great Britain struck it down a few years ago, was at once the blot upon our civilization and the chronic danger of the Empire.

The total quantity of land in Lower Canada granted to the seigniors exceeded twelve million superficial "arpents," or about 15,390 miles.* There is nothing more remarkable in our past political history than the fact that the King of England, at one time, desired to extend over and perpetuate in Canada this seigniorial system, with all its manifold burdens and effective impediments to immigration and the development of the country. In the year 1775, the King, in the 38th Article of his Instructions to Governor Carleton, commanded as follows:— "It is, therefore, our will and pleasure that all the lands which now are or hereafter will be subjected to our disposal, be granted in *fief* or *seigneurie* in like manner as was practised antecedent to the Conquest." Later still, in 1786, in the 40th Article of the Royal Instructions to Carleton—by this time created Lord Dorchester—the King again pronounces in favour of the feudal tenures. His Majesty, after directing that the exiled Loyalists from the United States, and the disbanded troops, should re-

---

* Bouchette, "Hist. Can." (1832), vol. i. p. 380.

ceive grants of the waste lands of the Crown, ordered that these lands should be held *en seigneurie*. These same men, all this time, were making every possible exertion to obtain from the Mother Country the abolition of the feudal, and the establishment of freehold, tenures. But it was not until the year 1789 that the tenure of free and common soccage was effectually introduced. A French Canadian historian says—" Notwithstanding these repeated and powerful manifestations of the Crown to perpetuate the tenure of fief and seigniory in Lower Canada, . . . no fresh grants in fief were made after the Conquest, if we except those of Shoolbred and Murray Bay; and the whole of the lands of the Colony not previously granted under the feudal system are now considered as soccage lands."*

It is well in this place to bear in mind that at this period, and until the passing of the Constitutional Act of 1791, the Province of Quebec comprised the territory which by that Act was set apart as Upper Canada. It was in this western portion of Quebec, afterwards the Province of Upper Canada, that the Loyalists who were expelled from the United States by the men in arms against the King, chose to seek new homes, and to found a new Britain. To these men, who had suffered and lost so much for the unity of the Empire, the feudal tenure was a grievance to the full as galling as some of those to avoid which they had turned their backs upon civilization, and set their faces toward the wilderness.

* Bouchette, vol. I. p. 876.

## CHAPTER XIV.

### THE CANADIAN REIGN OF TERROR.

In the tempest and turmoil of the American Invasion, the doors of the Legislative Council were shut against the appeals of the people of Canada. But the footprint of the last flying enemy had scarcely been effaced from our soil, when the jaws of the prisons opened for the eternal prey of tyranny—the bolder spirits of the land.

It was not until 1777, the second year after the American Invasion, that the Legislative Council reassembled. But the popular voice found no kindly echo within its walls. The functions of this body were of a double nature : they were self-seeking as regarded itself, despotic in respect to the people. There was little difference, in this respect, between the British and the French Canadian Councillors. The former numbered fifteen, and the latter eight; and all were salaried. The British clamoured for advantageous grants of land : the French members demanded, " as men of noble rank, all sorts of aristocratic privileges. . . . They were always in opposition to the people's interests, when these interfered in any way with their own immunities."[*]
They believed only in military government. They worshipped Power, and were its unreasoning slaves, except

[*] Garneau, "Hist. Can.," vol. ii. p. 166.

when it put forth its hand against their order or their nationality.*

. When the Council met, it was not to seek remedies for the healing of the country, but to forge fetters for its limbs, as yet bleeding and paralyzed. An ordinance was passed, creating a military despotism. All the inhabitants were compelled to submit to the unquestioning tyranny of the sword. They were to bear arms beyond the Canadian frontiers for an unlimited period, and were not even to receive the scanty pittance of the soldier. For those absent on military service, they who chanced to be at home were obliged to undertake agricultural labour, and this without any manner of reward. For neglect or refusal of the commands of this ordinance, the people were subjected to the most severe penalties.

The Council, in addition to the military code, passed other ordinances. They introduced the commercial code of England and established a Court of Probate. They constituted themselves a Court of Appeal, but left a final power of appeal to the Privy Council in England: they authorized the opening of Courts of Oyer and Terminer.

The labours of the Council engendered social and political chaos. The tribunals administered law, sometimes according to the French, at other times according to the English code. But the militia law was the greatest calamity; it weighed down to the very earth

* Garneau, " Hist. Can.," vol. ii. p. 166.

the miserable peasantry. The British colonists were the spokesmen for their oppressed fellow-citizens as well as for themselves; but just as they had taken the first step to compel the Legislative Council to listen to the complaints of the Province, a new and hostile influence brought itself to bear on Canada. In 1777, General Haldimand, by birth a Swiss, by profession a soldier in the British army, replaced Carleton in the Governorship of the Province. Under his sway, the natural antagonism between liberty and the rule of the sword displayed itself in all of its unrelenting and repulsive phases. Haldimand acted as if the people of Canada were the rank and file of a mutinous regiment. The spectre of Republicanism haunted him by day and terrified him by night. Imprisonment—reckless, needless, cruel— was his sole exorcism. The enforced military service, and the enforced statute labour, wore out the bodies and the patience of the peasantry. They could do nothing but complain. But to tyrants, in troublous times, complaint is held to be akin to treason. Haldimand fancied that these lamentations were the outpourings of the spirit of revolt, excited by republican emissaries. He tried to stifle them in the dumbness of the dungeon. Acting on mere suspicion, he filled the prisons with multitudes, indifferent as to whether they were innocent or guilty.*

The Council looked upon these outrages with pitiless

* Garneau, "Hist. Can.," vol. ii. p. 170.

eyes and callous hearts. In 1779 it met, sat for a few days: renewed some ordinances about to expire: adjourned. In 1780 it again assembled. One of its members, named Allsopp, moved that the Governor should be asked for a copy of his Instructions respecting the administration of the Province. The proposition was voted down. The outcry of the people was not, however, to be altogether silenced, even in the Council. Again Mr. Allsopp, who was in opposition to the despotism of the time, demanded the introduction of the free laws of Great Britain. But once more he was doomed to fail. A rumour had gone abroad that the Americans were preparing for another invasion. The Government became more tyrannical. That cruelty which is the sure sign of weakness and of rottenness in a state, was again put forth in military arrests. The rich and the poor alike, on the mere suspicion of treason, on charges for lesser offences, and no accusation whatever, were swept before a wave of bayonets into the filled and festering prisons, or into the noisome holds of war-vessels in the St. Lawrence. No information was vouchsafed to these miserable men as to the cause for which they had been robbed of their liberty. Many suffered not only loss of liberty, but of fortune.*

The Government of Canada reached the shameful summit of its tyranny in respect to its treatment of private correspondence. Matters of a private nature,

* Garneau, "Hist. Can.," vol. ii. pp. 173, 174.

which, on account of their very privacy, assume, by the general consent of men and moralists, a character almost sacred, were violated by the polluted fingers of the robber-spy. On several occasions the European mail-bags were found lying opened at the Governor's, and the contents scattered about the floor.* The distrust in which Governor Haldimand held letter-writers was encouraged by the seigniorial members of the Council, who feared that Republicanism, if it succeeded in Canada, would trample their privileges in the dust.† The principal pretexts for these multiplied outrages were mere suspicion of being in communication with the Americans, and disobedience to the new militia law. As a rule, the French Canadians, in greater numbers than the British, were made to feel the tyranny of Governor Haldimand and his Legislative Council.

* Garneau, "Hist. Can.," vol. ii. p. 173.
† Ibid.

# CHAPTER XV.

PEACE BETWEEN GREAT BRITAIN AND THE UNITED STATES: ITS EFFECTS ON CANADA.

The treaty of peace concluded between Great Britain and the United States on the 3rd of September, 1783, was the talisman that set the Canadian state prisoners free. The jails disgorged the victims of arbitrary arrests, innocent or guilty. But Governor Haldimand and the Legislative Council gave to these sufferers neither the melancholy satisfaction of knowing wherefore they had been deprived of their liberty, nor indemnity for the deprivation. The treaty of peace stripped Canada of the five western countries which had been added to it by the Quebec Act. The United States, characterized even then by the territorial gluttony which they have ever since displayed for the possessions of their neighbours, clamoured for and closed upon Lake Champlain, an important adjunct and defence of Eastern or Lower Canada.

If the treaty narrowed the boundaries of Canada, it brought her peace. With peace came the dawn of personal liberty. In 1785, the British Ministry chose to indicate to the rulers of Canada that it was now time to revive the slumbering writ of *habeas corpus*. But the Legislative Council must needs debate the matter. This body, which was swift of deed when the rights of the men of Canada were to be violated, was slow of deed, even when called upon by the Ministers of the Empire, to make atonement. The Council, however, dared not long resist the behests of the Mother Country and the pressure of Provincial popular opinion, which, gathering strength in Canada, was rolling up like a wave against the barricaded doors of the Legislative conclave. The Council were obliged to pass an ordinance introducing the law of *habeas corpus.* Governor Haldimand signed the instrument. It was his last official act. He left Canada, pursued by the hot indignation of the vast majority of the inhabitants of both races.* The people could not believe that they had been oppressed by the will and wish of the Mother Country. Upon Haldimand, therefore, who, in reality, was no more to blame than the Legislative Council, if indeed he were to blame as much, the people of Canada joined in pouring out the vial of national hatred, a stream which keeps fresh, for ever, the tainted memory of him on whom it has once descended. It must be said, however, in justice to Haldimand, that his despotism had but one object in view: to prevent Canada from falling into the jaws of the United States.

* Aware that he was detested by the people, Haldimand, during his last two years of office, repeatedly solicited his recall.—Garneau, "Hist. Can.," vol. ii. p. 180.

# CHAPTER XVI.

THE PEOPLE ENTREAT FOR CONSTITUTIONAL GOVERN-
MENT.—OPPOSITION OF THE LEGISLATIVE COUNCIL.—
DEPLORABLE CONDITION OF CANADA.

As soon as the weight of military despotism was removed from the Province, there followed the natural rebound. The British and French Canadians, in 1783, united themselves in petitions to the Home Government, praying for constitutional changes, for equal political rights, for a House of Assembly, for the restoration of the law of *habeas corpus*. The Legislative Council became alarmed. In 1784, by a majority of two-thirds, it passed an address to the King, thanking him for his protection during the American war, and praying that he would permit no change in the mode of government established by the Quebec Bill. This address, which was merely the echo of a paltry minority of the people of Canada, had the effect, when it reached England, of postponing the day of constitutional government. Lord Sidney, one of the principal Secretaries of State, was content that the law of *habeas corpus* should be introduced ; but he was of opinion that those who demanded a Legislative Assembly, trial by jury, and the permanence of the seats of the judges, were persons of evil dispositions and of ques-

F

tionable loyalty.* The people of Canada, however, were not thus to be silenced. Montreal and Quebec, in 1784, petitioned for an elective Assembly, a Council of unsalaried members, the extension of British jurisprudence to places not yet organized for judicial purposes, and trial by jury in civil cases. Counter-petitions from the party of tyranny followed the others to London. The British Ministry were perplexed. Some of the propositions belonged to that class of which the novelty obscures, for the moment, the underlying absurdity. One petition, for example, prayed that the British inhabitants should be represented in the House of Commons, stating that this would be much better than to establish a Colonial Assembly, whose members, French Canadians, would be elected by their co-nationalists.

The war of petitions and counter-petitions was waged from 1785 to 1788. The British House of Commons gave them passing notice, but not practical consideration; for the affairs of Europe were filling, to the exclusion of all else, every sphere of legislation. In 1789, Mr. Grenville, successor to Lord Sidney, transmitted to Lord Dorchester, Governor-General of Canada, the scheme of a constitution. Mr. Grenville further requested the Governor to send home to England the views which, after mature consideration, he might form concerning the whole matter.

The social condition of Canada, in the period between

* Garneau, " Hist. Can.," vol. ii. p. 168.

the American Invasion and 1787, was deplorable. Society seemed to be in danger of dissolving into its primitive barbaric elements. Liberty, justice, security, there were none. An inquiry, carried out in 1787 by Lord Dorchester, at the command of the British Government, threw some gleams of light on the seething social chaos. The worst of the revelations was, that the fountain of justice was polluted at its source. One judge had been seen, when drunk, to ascend the bench, and disgrace the administration of the law. The same judge had often refused to hear evidence, stating that outside of the Court he had been in communication with the litigants. Another judge, in order to nonsuit a party in a case, himself produced a letter from an individual interested in the action, which letter, denying certain facts, the judge accepted for evidence. In another case, the same judge stopped the suit, simply observing that he knew the defendant, and that he was a man quite incapable of the act of which he stood charged. Worst of all, perhaps, it was ascertained that Governor Haldimand, himself, on one occasion took his seat on the bench, and, by influencing the judges, had caused M. du Calvet, a political prisoner, to be despoiled of the sum of £6,000.

The intellectual condition of the people was wretched. An ignorance, like that Egyptian darkness which could be felt, was spread over the whole land, making the minds of men barren, sluggish and unwholesome. No system of elementary education had been provided for the people. There was not a public school-house in the

Province. Nor, in the matter of the repression of crime, was there any effective agency. A court-house did not exist in Canada ; nor was there a serviceable prison nor a house of correction in the country. Such was the condition of things when the British Parliament reached forth its hand to Canada, to lead her up the steep and hazardous way that ascends to Constitutional Government.

## CHAPTER XVII.

#### THE NATION-BUILDERS OF UPPER CANADA.

In the period previous to the rupture between Great Britain and her Colonies, and during the progress of the struggle, there were those in the disaffected Provinces who sympathised with the Mother Country. These men were, as a rule, amongst the most estimable of the population. To their revolted fellow-citizens, the feelings which actuated these Loyalists ought to have been a guarantee for respect, or, at least, ought to have pleaded for a generous forbearance. For these friends of British connection were no unreasoning lovers of tyranny. But they believed, in all honesty of heart, that there was no cause why the Thirteen Colonies should break away from Great Britain. They chose an heroic part; they would not let the self-interest of the moment bear down, and bury out of sight for ever, the warm and well-earned remembrance of all the past kindnesses which the Mother Land had heaped upon her offspring. The present unreasonable demands of the Parent could not extinguish the kindly flame of gratitude which fed itself on the hearts of the American Loyalists.

These men were in a minority, the invariable fate of moderation in any great political problem. The majority of their countrymen rose up against them. To the tiger-passions of the mob, thirst for blood, and cruelty for the sake of cruelty, were added, in the case of the outnumbered Loyalists, lust for their possessions, with that unreasoning hatred which is the certain outcome of civil war, and sure to be engendered between brethren of the aforetime. Some of the Loyalists took up arms in defence of King, Parliament and a United Empire. In the case of the aged and the non-combatants ; in the case of that denomination of Christian men whose glory it is to walk the world searching for the blessing pronounced by the Divine lips two thousand years ago on the peacemakers—in the case of all these, the outrages of civil war were unleashed like so many blood-hounds.*

These Loyalists, like wild beasts, were hunted out of their native land. They fled to Canada, they and their wives and their little ones. The savage wilderness gave them shelter from their more savage brethren. They chose the Western portion of Canada as the place where they would hew out for themselves a rude and wretched resemblance of that home from which they had been driven. The Mother Country did not forget those who, for her sake, had become exiles. Lands were granted to them ; they were taken under the special protection of the Empire. And, in 1789, an Order in Council testified to their worthiness of Imperial favour and permanent recognition. "To put a mark of honour upon the families who had adhered to the unity of the Empire, and joined the Royal standard in America, before the Treaty of Separation, in 1783," the Order in Council commanded

* See Lorenzo Sabine's "History of the United Empire Loyalists."

that a list of these men should be prepared. This was to be done in order that "their posterity might be discriminated from the then future settlers." The initials in the words of the Order in Council, "Unity of the Empire," gave to this roll of honour the appellation of the "U. E." List. The immediate offspring of those whose names were thus inscribed, reaped advantage from the circumstance. And, in the war of 1812, they proved to the world that these favours had been well bestowed, and that the ancestral valour of their race had not become degenerate.

It must not be supposed that these expatriated colonists were the blind champions of arbitrary rule. They were the very opposite. They would have repudiated, with indignation, the slavish doctrine that the Monarch alone should make laws for Great Britain or the Colonies. They believed in the Constitution as then interpreted—namely, that the King, Lords and Commons of right had, and ought to have, supreme legislative sovereignty over all colonies of English-speaking men. The idea which fed the conflict of Great Britain with her Colonies was not so much that the King should have domination, as that this domination should belong to Parliament. The annals of our British Parliaments are an anomalous and a conflicting record. In respect to our whole legislative history, the feelings of the Nation have oscillated between two extremes—superstitious reverence and loud-spoken contempt. At this period, the feeling of reverence happened to be in the ascendant. Parliament, which is as the brain of the body politic, and occasionally in magnetic sympathy with the moods and passions of the hour, chanced, at this epoch, to be thrilled and influenced by the national impulse towards war. The Loyalists in the Colonies were in unison with the majority of their fellow-citizens at Home, but in discord with the majority of their fellow-citizens in America.

The settlement of the Loyalists in Canada was worth more than an army to the British Colonists in the Eastern part of the Province, praying for a House of Assembly. The U. E Loyalists did not suffer for Great Britain with the intention of yielding up their hereditary right to Representative Government, and their privileges as British citizens. They were not long in Canada until they protested against the feudal tenures.* And, thinking they recognised social barriers that might, in the future, separate them, in many respects, from Eastern Canada, the U. E. Loyalists of the Western section were desirous of having a Legislature of their own, moulded, as nearly as possible, after the similitude of the Parliament of the Mother Land. Such were the men who were the Nation-Builders of Upper Canada; who laid, in heroism, self-sacrifice, loyalty and steadfast labour, the foundation of a social and political system which, of all the social and political systems in this New World, most nearly resembles that of Great Britain. From such beginning rose Ontario, the Pillar Province of the British North American Confederation.

* See ante, p. 8.

# CHAPTER XVIII.

CANADA IN THE BRITISH PARLIAMENT.—THE KING'S
MESSAGE.

On the 25th of February, 1791, in the House of Commons, William Pitt presented a message from His Majesty respecting the government of Quebec. The King acquainted the House that it appeared to him it would be for the benefit of his subjects in his Province of Quebec to divide it into two separate Provinces, the one to be called Upper, and the other Lower, Canada. Therefore, it was his intention so to divide Quebec, whenever he should be enabled, by Act of Parliament, to establish the necessary regulations for the government of the two Provinces. His Majesty, accordingly, recommended this object to the consideration of the House. He also recommended the consideration of such provisions as might be necessary to make a permanent appropriation of lands in the two Provinces for the support and maintenance of a Protestant clergy, the appropriation to be in proportion to such lands as he had already granted within the Provinces.*

On the 4th of March, the order of the day being read for taking into consideration His Majesty's message relative to the government of Quebec, William Pitt made a

* "Parliamentary History," vol. xxviii. p. 1271.

motion founded upon the message. The object of his motion was to repeal part of the Quebec Bill, and to enact new regulations for the future government of that Province. The new Bill was intended to put an end to the differences of opinion and growing competition for some years existing in Canada, on several important points, between the ancient inhabitants and the new settlers from England and from America; and to bring the government of the Province as near to the British Constitution as circumstances would admit.

The first great object of the new Bill was to divide the Province into two parts: one to be named Upper, the other Lower, Canada. The Upper Province was to be for the English and American settlers; the Lower, for the Canadians. The division, it was hoped, could be made in such a manner as to give to each race a great majority in its own particular territory. In each Province were to be established a House of Assembly and Legislative Council, which would give all the advantages of the British Constitution. Members of the Council would hold their seats, not during pleasure, but for life. Further, the descendants of such members as should be honoured with hereditary titles were to have an hereditary right of sitting in the Council. It was also proposed to annex the dignity of a member of Council to every title of honour that might be conferred.

The Canadians were in possession, in many respects, of the English civil law. But this law did not extend to landed property. It was therefore intended that landed property should rest on soccage tenures. A specific point in the Bill was the extension of the *Habeas Corpus* Act to both Provinces ; the Act was at present in operation in Canada, under the authority of a Provincial ordinance : and an ordinance had the force of law.

The laws in operation would be continued until the Assembly of each Province chose to alter them. In this manner, the complaints of the petitions now before the House would be remedied, as the inhabitants of Quebec would have an Assembly, with the power of enacting what laws they pleased.

The Bill contained another important enactment. It made provision for the maintenance of the Protestant clergy in both Provinces. For this purpose there was to be a permanent appropriation of certain portions of land ; and such provisions for future grants of land within each Province, in proportion to the increase of their population and cultivation, as might best conduce to the same object. But, as in one of the Provinces the majority of the inhabitants would be Roman Catholics, it was meant to provide that it should not be lawful for His Majesty, in future, to assent to grants of land for this purpose, under the sanction of the Council and Assembly of either Province, without first submitting them to the consideration of the British Parliament.

In regard to taxation :—To avoid the occasion of a misunderstanding similar to that which had formerly taken place in respect to the Thirteen Colonies, no taxes were meant to be imposed by the British Parliament on Canada, saving only such as might be necessary for the purposes of commercial regulation. But in this case, so as to avoid even the possibility of a cavil, the levying and disposal of such taxes should be left entirely to the wisdom of the Provincial Legislatures.

By dividing the Province into two, Pitt conceived that the existing causes of controversy would be removed. " In the Lower Canada, as the residents would be chiefly Canadians, their Assembly would be adapted to their habits and prejudices. The Upper Canada, being almost entirely peopled by emigrants from Great Britain, or from America, the Protestant religion would be the Establishment, and they would have the benefit of the English tenure law." He moved for leave to bring in a Bill " to repeal certain parts of the Act 14 George 3rd, and to make further provision for the government of the said Province."*

Charles James Fox found it impossible to concur in any plan like the one proposed until the Bill was before the House. But he was willing to declare that the giving to a country so far distant from England a Legislature, and the power of governing for itself, would exceedingly prepossess him in favour of every part of the plan. He did not hesitate to say, that if a Local Legislature were liberally formed, that circumstance would incline him much to overlook defects in the other regulations. For he was

* "Parliamentary History," vol. xxviii. pp. 1376–1379.

convinced that the only means of retaining distant colonies with advantage was to enable them to govern themselves.*

Pitt obtained leave to bring in the Bill.

* "Parliamentary History," vol. xxviii. p. 1379.

# CHAPTER XIX.

### THE BRITISH MERCHANTS IN EASTERN CANADA OPPOSE THE BILL.

The British merchants in Eastern Canada took exception to several propositions in the Bill. On the 23rd of March, 1791, Mr. Adam Lymburner, a Quebec colonist, and their agent, was heard on their behalf at the bar of the House of Commons.

The House of Commons heard from the Canadian agent some of the grievances of the Quebec Bill. The people had severely felt and suffered under the confusion which that Bill had introduced. They had been exposed to the pernicious effects of uncertain and undefined laws, and to the arbitrary judgments of Courts guided by no fixed principles and certain rules. What was called in the Quebec Bill "the Laws of Canada" had not yet been defined. Sixteen years had now elapsed since that Bill came into effect; but it was not determined what or how many of the laws of France composed the system of Canadian jurisprudence previous to the Conquest; or even if there were any positive system, particularly for commercial transactions. He stood before the House as the agent of a number of the most respectable and intelligent of the French Canadians, to solicit the total repeal of the Quebec Bill.

The investigation made by order of Lord Dorchester, in 1787, into the past administration of justice in the Province, as well as the disputes between the Upper and Lower Courts since that period, showed that neither the judges, the lawyers nor the people understood what were the laws of Canada previous to the Conquest. There had been no certainty on any object of litigation except in such matters as regarded the possession, transmission or alienation of landed property where the Custom of Paris was very clear.

On behalf of those he represented, Mr. Lymburner opposed the intention of the new Act to divide Quebec into two Provinces. He had not heard this had been the general wish of the Loyalists who had settled in the Upper or Western part of the Province; it was not the desire of the people of the Lower or Eastern part. The Loyalists, as well as the inhabitants of Eastern Quebec, had had reason to complain of the present system of Civil Government. But, even supposing the Loyalists had wished for a division of the Province, he hoped the House would consider that, in a matter of such vast importance as the separation for ever of the interests and connections of those who, from local situation, were certainly designed by nature to remain united, that the interest, the feelings and desires of Eastern Quebec ought to be consulted. Deference in this respect was as much owing to Eastern Quebec as to the wild project of a small body of people who were thinly scattered over the upper parts of the Province, and who had not had time to examine into their relative situation, and the natural dependence which their country must have on the lower parts of the Province.* As an additional argument against separation, he stated that, in petitions then on the table of the House, the people of Eastern Quebec had complained that already the Province had been greatly mutilated, and that its resources would be greatly reduced by the operation of the Treaty of Peace of 1783.

To that portion of the Bill which provided for a Canadian hereditary peerage or aristocracy, Mr. Lymburner offered a determined opposition. The people, as would be seen from the petitions on the table, had only requested that the Legislative Councillors should hold their offices during life. The hereditary principle was an expedient extremely dangerous in any infant colony; but it must appear absolutely ridiculous in the Province of Quebec, where there were so few landed estates of any considerable value; and where, by the laws of inheritance, these estates must, at every succession, be reduced to one-half, and in two generations inevitably sink into insignificance. Thus, the hereditary Councillors, from their poverty, would become objects of contempt to the public. It might be said that the families of Legislative Councillors might be supported in an independent situation by introducing the laws of primogeniture. But this would be extremely injurious to the Province. The French law, in this respect,

---

* Mr. Lymburner was somewhat inconsistent with himself. He had just previously stated that he had not heard that separation "had been the general wish of the Loyalists."

was much better calculated for a young country, where it was of great advantage to cultivation and population that landed property should be divided, fluctuate and change owners. He informed the House that, poor as the country really was, on account of the oppressive system of laws under which it had suffered, there were, amongst its merchants, those whose moveable fortunes were, perhaps, equal, if not superior, to any of the seigniorial estates. These men, from the employment and support they gave to thousands of the people, had infinitely more influence in the country than the seigniors. For it would not be difficult to prove that the seigniors were almost universally disliked by their tenants. From these facts he hoped the House would see the impropriety and the danger of rendering the office of Councillor hereditary.*

Mr. Lymburner pointed out what he considered had been a radical defect in the representation of all our American Colonies. There were but few towns in the Colonies. These towns had only their proportion of representatives. The result was, that the landed interest had always been too prevalent, and had, at times, greatly oppressed the commerce of the Colonies, and impeded the operations of government.

He entreated that the Province should not, for some time, be called upon to defray the expenses of its civil

---

* Mr. Lymburner's argument had no effect. The Bill established the hereditary principle. But no Governor, in either Province, ever ventured to give it effect. The Governors knew Canada better than British Ministers or Parliaments.

Government. He acknowledged it was the intention of his constituents that the Province should defray these expenses. But Canada had been so long oppressed and neglected, and every object of industry and improvement had been so apparently discouraged, that the country was now reduced to such a state of languor and depression, that it was unable to provide for the expenses of its Civil Government. This present financial inability ought to be excused in those who had been told " that ignorance and poverty were the best security for the obedience of the subject; and that those who did not approve of these political principles might leave the country." He hoped, therefore, that the House of Commons would release the Province of the expenses of the Civil List for a certain number of years.‡

Mr. Lymburner asked, on behalf of his constituents: The total repeal of the Quebec Act: that optional juries might be granted in civil cases, nine jurors out of twelve being sufficient to return a verdict. That the judges might not be subject to suspension or removal by the Governor. Amongst the objections Mr. Lymburner made to the Bill were the claiming of tithes from the distant Protestant settlers, and not fixing the rate. The House refused to concede the requests, or to entertain the objection.

‡ The House of Commons granted the request of Mr. Lymburner, and dealt "most liberally, at least, with respect to Lower Canada. It was not until 1818 that the Assembly of this Province was called upon, pursuant to their voluntary offer in 1810, to vote the necessary expenses of the Civil Government."—Christie, Hist. L. C., vol. i., p. 103.

## CHAPTER XX.

FOX AND PITT ON THE NEW CONSTITUTION.

In the House of Commons, on the 8th of April, Mr. Hussey presented a petition from several merchants concerned in the trade to Quebec, praying that the Quebec Government Bill might not pass. The petition stated that the Bill would be attended with great injury to the Province, and particularly to the trade and commerce of the petitioners. The Speaker having put the question, " that the Report of the Committee on the Bill be now taken into further consideration," Mr. Hussey moved that the Bill be re-committed.*

Charles James Fox then rose in his place to second the motion. He thought that a Constitution should be framed for Canada as consistent as possible with the principles of freedom. This Bill would not establish such a Government, and that was his chief reason for opposing it. He approved of a House of Assembly for each Province ; but the number of members deserved particular attention. Although it might be perfectly true that a country three or four times as large as Great Britain ought to have representatives three or four times as numerous, yet it was not fit to say that a small country should have an Assembly proportionally small. The

* "Parliamentary History," vol. xxix. p. 105.

great object in the institution of all popular assemblies was, that the people should be freely and fully represented, and that the representative body should have all the virtues and the vices incidental to such assemblies. But when they made an assembly to consist of sixteen or thirty persons, they gave a free Constitution in appearance, when, in fact, they withheld it.

He opposed the proposition of the Bill to make the Canadian Legislatures septennial ; and thought that, from the situation of Canada, annual or triennial Parliaments would be much preferable. He disapproved of the electoral qualification. In England, a freehold of forty shillings was sufficient ; in Canada, five pounds were necessary. This might be said to make no material difference. But, granting that it did not ; when the House was giving to the world, by this Bill, its notions of the principles of election, it should not hold out that the qualifications in Great Britain were lower than they ought to be. The qualification on a house in Canada was to be ten pounds. In fact, he thought that the whole of this Constitution was an attempt to undermine and contradict the professed purport of the Bill—namely, the introduction of a Popular Government into Canada.

He pointed out this anomaly: that although the Legislative Assemblies were to consist of so inconsiderable a representation, the Legislative Councils were unlimited as to numbers. He saw nothing so good in hereditary powers and honours as to incline the House to introduce them into a country where they were unknown, and

CONSTITUTIONAL HISTORY OF CANADA. 109

by such means distinguish Canada from all the Colonies on the other side of the Atlantic. In countries where they made a part of the Constitution, he did not think it wise to destroy them; but to give birth and life to such principles in countries where they did not exist, appeared to him to be exceedingly unwise. Nor could he account for it, unless it was that Canada having been formerly a French colony, there might be an opportunity of reviving those titles of honour, the extinction of which some gentlemen so much deplored.* It seemed to him peculiarly absurd to introduce hereditary honours in America, where those artificial distinctions stunk in the nostrils of the natives. He thought these powers and honours wholly unnecessary, and tending rather to make a new Constitution worse than better. If the Council were wholly hereditary, he should equally object to it: it would only add to the power of the King and Governor. For a Council so constituted would only be the tool of the Governor, as the Governor himself would only be the tool and engine of the King.

The enactment respecting the reservation of lands for ecclesiastical purposes, next provoked the criticism of Fox. He totally disapproved of the clause which provided, "that whenever the King shall make grants of lands, one-seventh part of those lands shall be appropriated to the Protestant clergy." He had two objections to these regulations. In all grants of lands made in that country

* The allusion was to the overthrow of the aristocracy of France by the recent Revolution.

to Catholics—and a majority of the inhabitants were of that persuasion—one-seventh part of those grants was to be appropriated to the Protestant clergy, although they might not have any cure of souls, or any congregation to instruct. One-tenth part of the produce of this country was assigned, and this, perhaps, was more than one-seventh part of the land. He wished to deprive no clergyman of his just rights; but in settling a new constitution, to enact that the clergy should have one-seventh of all grants appeared to him an absurd doctrine. If they were all of the Church of England, this would not reconcile him to the measure. The greater part of these Protestant clergy were not of the Church of England; they were chiefly Protestant Dissenters. The House was therefore going to give Dissenters one-seventh of all the lands in the Province. This was not the proportion either in Scotland or in any other country where those religious principles were professed. This provision would rather tend to corrupt than to benefit the clergy.

Fox complained that, with all its variety of clauses and regulations, there had not yet been a word said in explanation of the Bill. It went through the House silently, without one observation; it also went through the Committee, only in form, but not in substance.

He proceeded to discuss that enactment of the Bill which struck him the most forcibly. This was the division of the Province of Canada. It had been urged that, by such means, the House could separate the English and French inhabitants of the Province. But was this to be desired? Was it not rather to be avoided? Was it agreeable to general political expediency? The most desirable circumstance was, that the French and English inhabitants should unite and coalesce, as it were, into one body, and that the different distinctions of the people might be extinguished for ever. If this had been the object in view, the English laws might soon have prevailed universally throughout Canada, not from force, but from choice and conviction of their superiority. The inhabitants of Canada had not the laws of France. The Commercial Code was not established there; they stood upon the exceedingly inconvenient Custom of Paris. He wished the people of the country to adopt the English laws from choice, and not from force; and he did not think the division of the Province the most likely thing to bring about this desirable end. Canada was a country as capable of enjoying political freedom as any other country on the face of the globe. It was material that the inhabitants should have nothing to look to among their neighbours to excite their envy. Canada must be preserved to Great Britain by the choice of its inhabitants. But it should be felt by the inhabitants that their situation was not worse than that of their neighbours. This, however, would never be the case under a Bill which held out to them something like the shadow of the British Constitution, but denied them the substance. He held that the Legislative Councils ought to be totally free, and repeatedly chosen; in a manner as much independent of the Governor as the nature of the Colony would admit. But if not, they should have their seats for life; be appointed by the King; consist of a limited number, and possess no hereditary honours.*

William Pitt confessed it was certainly his wish that the Assemblies in both Provinces might prove numerous enough to answer all the purposess of a Popular Assembly, as far as the circumstances of the two Provinces were properly qualified for that situation. But he doubted very much, according to the present state of the Colony and its population, whether the Assemblies could be rendered more numerous than was proposed. There was no wish that the Assemblies should not be increased, when the population of the Province increased. The Assemblies, undoubtedly, ought to be extended with the growing population of Canada. He believed that a very numerous representative body was in no respect desirable, and that they ought always to bear some proportion to the circumstances of the country.

A House of Assembly for seven years would surely be better than one for a shorter period. In the other Colonies, the Councils and Assemblies were constituted in such a manner as to invest the Governor with more influence than would be given him by the present Bill. If the Assemblies were not properly constituted at first, it must be recollected that there was a remedy. There was nothing to hinder the Parliament of Great Britain from correcting anything that might hereafter appear to want correction.

* "Parliamentary History," vol. xxix. pp. 104-111.

Pitt entirely differed from Fox in the opinion that the Legislative Council should be elective. An aristocratical principle being one part of our Mixed Government, he thought it proper that there should be such a Council in Canada as was provided for by the Bill, and which might answer to that part of the British Constitution composed by the other House of Parliament.

He defended the appropriation of lands for the support of the clergy. If one-seventh turned out to be too much in future, the matter, like everything else in the Bill, was subject to a revision. It was to be recollected that one-seventh had almost grown into an established custom, where land had been given in commutation for tithes. One-tenth of the produce, which took place in England, must be confessed to be a far greater provision than one-seventh of land.

The division of the Province, Pitt declared, was in a great measure the fundamental part of the Bill. He agreed with Fox that it was extremely desirable that the inhabitants of Canada should be united, and led universally to prefer the English Constitution and the English laws. To divide the Province was the most likely means to effect this purpose; since, by so doing, the French subjects would be sensible that the British Government had no intention of forcing the English laws upon them. Therefore, the French colonists would, with more facility, look at the operation and effect of those laws, compare them with the operation and effect of their own, and probably in time adopt them from conviction. This was more likely to be the case than if the British Government were all at once to subject the whole inhabitants to the Constitution and laws of England. Experience would teach them that the English laws were best; but he admitted that the French Colonists ought to be governed to their satisfaction.

If the Province were not divided, there would be only one House of Assembly. There being two parties, if those parties were equal, or nearly equal, in the Assembly, it would be the source of perpetual faction: if one of the parties were much stronger than the other, the other might justly claim that they were oppressed. It was on this persuasion that the division of the Province was conceived to be the most likely way of attaining every desirable end.

After the reply of Pitt, the Bill was ordered to be recommitted.*

On the 6th of May the Bill went into Committee, and was fully debated, clause by clause. On the 16th of the same month the report of the Committee was brought up.

Fox divided the House on the clause providing for hereditary legislators. For the negative he obtained 39 votes; Pitt, for the affirmative, received 88. Fox opposed the clause limiting to thirty the number of representatives for the Lower Canada Assembly. He proposed that the number should be a hundred. Pitt moved to leave out the word "thirty" and to insert "fifty."

* "Parliamentary History," vol. xxix. p.p. 111-113.

CONSTITUTIONAL HISTORY OF CANADA. 115

Fox objected to this number as still insufficient, and divided the House. But his amendment was lost: Yeas, 40; Noes, 91. The amendment of Pitt was inserted in the Bill.*

The King, on the 16th of August, 1791, gave his assent to the measure.

* "Parliamentary History," vol. xxix. pp. 429, 430.

# CHAPTER XXI.

### THE CONSTITUTIONAL ACT—1791.

The measure known in Canadian History as the "Constitutional Act," contained no fewer than fifty sections. Stripped of all technical wordiness, its more important provisions may be followed without wearisomeness.*

The Act opens with the confession, that the measure of 1774 was "in many respects inapplicable to the present condition and circumstances" of the Province. It was next declared "that it is expedient and necessary that further provision should now be made for the good government and prosperity of the Province." As an advance towards this result, so much of the Act of 1774 as related to the appointment of a Council for the affairs of the Province, or to the powers granted to that Council, was repealed.

The Act divided Quebec into Upper and Lower Canada. To each Province was given a Legislature, to be composed of a Legislative Council and an Assembly. To constitute the Council, the Governor of each Province was empowered to summon "a sufficient number of discreet and proper persons": from Upper Canada, no fewer than seven; from Lower Canada, no fewer than fifteen.

---

\* The Act is the 31st George 3rd, c. 31, (1791). Its title: "An Act to Repeal certain parts of an Act passed in the 14th year of His Majesty's reign, intituled 'An Act for making more effectual provision for the government of the Province of Quebec, in North America.'"

No person under twenty-one years of age was to be summoned to the Council; nor any one who was not a natural-born subject of the King, nor naturalized by Act of the British Parliament, or who had not become a subject by the Conquest and Cession of Canada. A seat in the Legislative Council was to be for life.

The Act then entered upon an attempt to lay the foundation of a future Canadian aristocracy. It was provided that whenever the King should think proper to confer, by Letters Patent under the Great Seal of either Province, any hereditary title of honour, descendible according to any course of descent limited in such Letters Patent, His Majesty might annex thereto, by the said Letters Patent, an hereditary right of being summoned to the Legislative Council of such Province. Every person on whom such right should be conferred, or to whom it should descend, was to be entitled to demand from the Governor his writ of summons to such Legislative Council.

The Governors were empowered to appoint and remove the Speakers of the Legislative Councils.

The whole number of members to be chosen for Upper Canada were not to be less than sixteen; for Lower Canada, not less than fifty.

For districts, or counties, or "circles," the electoral qualification was : That each voter should be possessed of lands held in freehold, or in fief, or in roture, or by certificate of the Governor and Council of the Province of Quebec. The lands were to be of the yearly value of forty shillings sterling or upwards, over and above all rents and charges.

The electoral qualification for towns or townships was: That each voter should be possessed of a dwelling-house and lot, held by the tenure already described. The yearly value of such property was to be five pounds sterling or upwards. Or, these conditions being absent, a person who had been a resident in a town or township for twelve months before the date of the writ of summons for the election, and who had paid one year's rent for his dwelling, at the rate of ten pounds sterling per annum or upwards, was entitled to a vote.

No person was capable of being elected a member of the Legislative Assemblies, who should be a member of either of the Legislative Councils; or a minister of the Church of England, or a minister, priest, ecclesiastic or teacher, either according to the rites of the Church of Rome, or any other form or profession of religious faith or worship.

No person, unless twenty-one years of age, and a British subject, could vote for a member of the Assembly, or hold a seat in that body. No person could vote for a member, or sit as one, who had been attainted for treason or felony in any court of law within any of the King's dominions.

The Governors were empowered to prorogue the Legislatures, and to dissolve the Legislative Assemblies, whenever they deemed it expedient. The Legislature in each Province was to be summoned once at least in every

CONSTITUTIONAL HISTORY OF CANADA. 119

twelve months. Every Assembly was to continue four years from the day of the return of the writs, and no longer : subject, nevertheless, to be sooner prorogued and dissolved by the Governor. No member of either House was to sit or vote until he took the oath of allegiance.

The Governors were to transmit, to the Secretary of State, copies of Bills to which their assent had been given. The King, in Council, might declare his disallowance of such Bills, within two years of receiving them. Bills reserved for the King's pleasure were not to have any force till his assent had been previously communicated to the Legislatures.\*

The Governor of each Province and the Executive Council were to be constituted a court of civil jurisdiction for hearing and determining appeals. But this enactment was made subject to the future action of the Legislatures.†

Provision was made "for the support of a Protestant clergy in each Province." In the Quebec Act of 1774, there was a clause which confirmed to the Roman Catholic clergy of that Province "their accustomed dues and rights with respect to such persons only as should profess the said religion." There was also added the condition, "that it should be lawful for His Majesty to make such provision out of the rest of the said accustomed dues and

\* All the preceding enactments, with the exception of the first, which relates to the abolition of the Council (created by the Act of 1774), were repealed by the Union Act (3-4 Vic. cap. 35, sec. 2).

† Other provisions, with regard to appeals, were afterwards made by the Legislatures of both Provinces, under the powers given by this section.

rights for the encouragement of the Protestant religion, and for the maintenance and support of a Protestant clergy within the said Province, as he should think necessary and expedient."

The present Act of 1791 having recited the above clause of the Act of 1774, went on to state : that, on the 3rd of January, 1775, the King, under his " Royal Sign Manual," directed that no incumbent professing the religion of the Church of Rome, appointed to any parish in the said Province, should be entitled to receive any tithes for lands or possessions occupied by a Protestant; but that such tithes should be received by such persons as the Governor should appoint. The tithes were to be reserved by the Receiver-General of the Province, for the support of a Protestant clergy to be actually resident within the same, and not otherwise.* All growing rents and profits of a vacant benefice were, during such vacancy, to be reserved and applied to the like uses.

The provisions of the Act of 1774, and those contained in the Royal Instructions of 1775, were now, by this Act of 1791, declared to remain and continue in full force and effect in each of the Provinces of Upper and Lower Canada. To the Legislatures of both Provinces power was given to vary or repeal the provisions of the Act of 1774, and those of the Royal Instructions. But this power was

* " Tithes were abolished in Upper Canada by 2 Geo. IV. cap. 32, and are not paid in Lower Canada by Protestants ; so that the section seems unlikely to have any effect, except as maintaining the Roman Catholic clergy in Lower Canada in their right to tithes from Roman Catholics."—"Consolidated Statutes of Canada," p. xvii. (1859).

only to be exercised under a certain restriction, to be afterwards mentioned. The present Act provided that the King might authorize the Governor of each Province to make allotments of land for the support of a Protestant clergy. The allotments were to be made out of the lands of the Crown, and were to "bear a due proportion" to the amount of lands which had in time past been granted by the Crown. All future grants were to carry with them "a proportionable allotment and appropriation of lands" for clerical purposes. No grant of land was to be "valid or effectual," unless containing a specification of the lands allotted for ecclesiastical uses. These clerical grants were to be, "as nearly as the circumstances and nature of the case would admit, of the like quality" as the secular grants which they accompanied. Further, they were to be equal in value to the seventh part of the secular lands. The rents arising from these ecclesiastical grants were to be devoted solely to the maintenance and support of a Protestant clergy.

It was further provided that the Governor, with the advice of the Executive Council, might erect parsonages, endow them, and present incumbents to them. The incumbents were to enjoy their benefices as in the case of the incumbents in England. The presentations to parsonages and the enjoyment of them were to be subject to the jurisdiction granted to the Bishop of Nova Scotia.*

* The Imperial Act 3–4 Vic. cap. 78, s. 11, repeals so much of the enactments just cited as relates to any such clerical land reservations thereafter to be made. The Provincial Act 14–15 Vic. cap. 175, repeals the enactments

H

The Legislative Council and Assembly of each Province were empowered to vary or repeal the provisions respecting the ecclesiastical lands. But it was provided that before such variation or repeal became law, it was to be laid before both Houses of Parliament in Great Britain. It was not to be lawful for the King to assent to such Act until thirty days after it had been laid before both Houses. Nor was it to be lawful for the King to give his assent in case either House of Parliament, within such thirty days, addressed him to withhold his assent.* The same reservation applied to the King's prerogative touching the granting of the waste lands of the Crown within the two Provinces.

In future all lands to be granted in Upper Canada were to be in free and common soccage; and the same privilege was to be extended to Lower Canada if the grantee so desired it. The privilege, however, was subject to such alterations with respect to the nature and consequences of such tenure of free and common soccage, as the Legislature of Lower Canada might choose to make.

relating to incumbencies, saving past rights if found valid, and directing how the presentation to any incumbency which is found to have been legally established, shall thereafter be made. The said Provincial Act was passed under the authority given in a section just cited, of the Act of 1791.—"Con. Stats. Can.," p. xvii.

* This section (the 42nd) of the Act of 1791, requiring that Bills respecting ecclesiastical rights and waste lands of the Crown should be reserved and laid before the Imperial Parliament, before receiving assent, was repealed by the Imperial Act 17-18 Vic. cap. 118, sec. 6. This enactment enables Her Majesty to assent to any Bill of the Canadian Legislature without its being laid before the Imperial Parliament; and the Governor to assent to any Bill without reserving it for the signification of Her Majesty's pleasure.—"Con. Stats. Can.," p. xviii.

The provision was inserted in the interest of the seigniorial tenures.

There was a clause which at length emancipated, from the feudal tenures, the settlers in Western Canada. It was enacted that any person in Upper Canada, holding his or her lands by virtue of any certificate of occupation derived under the authority of the Governor and Council of the Province of Quebec, and having power to alienate the same, might obtain a re-grant in free and common soccage.

The forty-sixth clause of the Act establishes a principle which, had it been conceded in season, might have preserved the Thirteen Colonies for the Empire. The clause was one of high importance to British America; for it pledged the faith of King, Lords and Commons to the renunciation of the taxing power, " except only such duties as it may be expedient to impose for the regulation of commerce."

The clause in question recites an Act passed in the 18th year of the King.* In this Act it was declared, " that the King and Parliament of Great Britain will not impose any duty, tax or assessment whatever, payable in any of His Majesty's Colonies, Provinces and Planta-

---

* This Act, intended to win back the revolted Thirteen Colonies to their allegiance, was entitled "An Act for removing all doubts and apprehensions concerning taxation by the Parliament of Great Britain in any of the Colonies, Provinces and Plantations in North America and the West Indies ; and for repealing so much of an Act made in the seventh year of the reign of his present Majesty as imposes a duty on tea imported from Great Britain into any Colony or Plantation in America, or relates thereto."

tions in North America or the West Indies, except only such duties as it may be expedient to impose for the regulation of commerce ; the net produce of such duties to be always paid and applied to and for the use of the Colony, Province or Plantation in which the same shall be respectively levied, in such manner as other duties collected by the authority of the respective general Courts or general Assemblies of such Colonies, Provinces and Plantations are ordinarily paid and applied."

This Act of 1791 now declares that it is necessary for the general benefit of the British Empire that such power of regulation of commerce should continue to be exercised by His Majesty, and the Parliament of Great Britain ; subject, nevertheless, to the condition hereinbefor reecited with respect to the application of any duties which may be imposed for that purpose.

It was then provided that nothing in this Act of 1791 should prevent the operation of any Act of Parliament establishing prohibitions or imposing duties for the regulation of navigation and commerce. And, further, that neither of the Provincial Legislatures should have power to vary or repeal any such law or laws, or in any manner to prevent or obstruct their execution. But the Act declared that the net produce of such duties should be applied to the use of the respective Provinces.

The Act concluded by providing that its powers should come into force not later than the 31st of December, 1791. Further, that the time for the issuing of the Writs

CONSTITUTIONAL HISTORY OF CANADA. 125

of Summons and Election should not be later than the 31st of December, 1792.

Pitt stated that the concession of the *Habeas Corpus* Act of England was to be a principal characteristic of the new Constitution. There is nothing in the Constitutional Act which, in express and precise language, guarantees *Habeas Corpus*. The Act only grants it in the terms of the thirty-second clause, which declares "that all laws, statutes and ordinances which shall be in force on the day to be fixed for the commencement of this Act within the said Provinces . . . shall remain and continue to be of the same authority and effect . . . as if this Act had not been made, and as if the said Province of Quebec had been divided." The *Habeas Corpus* Act was put in force by the ordinance of 1785. It was therefore a law when the Constitutional Act came into effect. But the clause gave the Legislature power to repeal or vary the laws, statutes and ordinances in force at the time it came into operation.

## CHAPTER XXII.

#### THE DEFECTS OF THE CONSTITUTIONAL ACT.

The marvellous political prescience of Charles James Fox was never, perhaps, so truly and so sadly exemplified as in the objections which he raised against the Constitutional Act. The greatest Liberal of his age seemed to stand, as it were, upon the mountain peak of the Constitution, and project his vision, clear with the light of political prophecy, forth like an arrow's flight, right into the far and misty Future. Almost everything to which he took exception proved, in the after years of Canadian history, a source of heartburning to the people, and of imminent peril to the State. He opposed a Legislative Council nominated by the Crown ; the appropriation of the public lands for ecclesiastical purposes ; the division of the Province and the consequent isolation of the inhabitants of both races. The first two of these questions were destined, for over half a century, to be the political plagues` of Canada, and the chronic perplexity of Great Britain. The third question is left to Time, the great alchemist who transmutes, in his slow, creative laboratory, the elements of doubt and danger of to-day into forces of safety in the hereafter.

William Pitt, in one respect, was no less a prophet than Fox. He defended his division of Canada on the ground that if there were but one Assembly, and parties nearly equal, there would be perpetual faction. The Federal system under which we live, the sixth experiment in government which Canada has made in the period between 1760 and 1867, is proof of the keen political foresight of the great Tory statesman.*

The Constitutional Act was a sop thrown to Canada: not a full constitutional concession. In all charity, the intent of the British Ministry must be conceived to have been good. But, in matters of government, the practical effect of an intent, good soever as the intent may be, is useless, worthless and wasted, if there be not taken into account the historical traditions, the immediate wants, the aspirations of a people. And, in the matter of aspirations, colonies, dependencies, weaker states—every race that has a Past—looks forward to and lives in the Future. The Constitutional Act failed to recognise these facts. It sought to dig round Canada a moat, guarded by the gibbering spectre of Mediævalism, to frighten back Liberty from her assault on privileges whose claim to pre-eminence was Age, not native and inherent excellence and utility.

The Constitutional Act failed the most mischievously in this, that under its future operations the people of Canada had no real and beneficial representation. There

* Our changes of government were: In 1760, Military Rule ; in 1763, the introduction of the laws of England ; in 1774, the Quebec Bill ; in 1791, the Constitutional Act ; in 1841, Union of Upper and Lower Canada ; in 1867, the Federal system.

was, it is true, in each Province a House of Assembly. But power it had none, except to give utterance to the grievances of the people. The Legislative Councils, nominated by the Crown, held the Legislative Assemblies by the throat, kept them prostrate and paralysed them.

The Act endeavoured to establish a Canadian aristocracy. But the effort failed. No Governor ever attempted to stand up against the twin-giants, the People and the Age, to do battle for this feudal anachronism. It is only where the bones and sweat of a score of generations of peasant-serfs fructify the soil, that the tree of aristocracy ever strikes root and finds nutriment. And here, in Canada, the free soil, unlike that of Europe in the past centuries, was destined for nobler purposes than to enslave the toiler in his life and forget him in his death. In a word, the Act was a body without a soul. It was a corpse, breathed upon by the breath of Authority, robed in the threadbare and discarded rags of the British Constitution, sent to Canada to be erected as an idol, where, after having stirred up hatreds for half a century, it was finally, with few tears and many rejoicings, buried out of sight, as the repulsive mummy of a principle dead for generations in the Mother Land.

Earl Russell, glancing at this portion of our history, says :*—

"In 1791, Mr. Pitt and Lord Grenville had given to that Province (Canada) an impracticable Constitu-

* See his work "On the English Government," Introduction, pp. lxvi.-lxvii.

tion. The Province was inhabited by Frenchmen of the age of Louis XIV., with no taint of the Revolution, and no mark of improvement. It should have been the task of the English Government to infuse into the province English freedom, English industry and English loyalty.

"Instead of that sensible course, it was the object of Mr. Pitt and Lord Grenville to separate English energy from French inertness; to shut up the industry of the English in the upper part of the colony, and to preserve the lower province as a sort of museum, where a French *noblesse*, with feudal titles and orders of knighthood, and tithes and seigniorial rights, might be preserved for ever as a memorial of the happiness of France before her Jacobin Revolution. But 'Fancy's fairy frostwork' melted away before the light of human progress. The titles and orders projected never were created; all fell into confusion."

With all deference to such a man as Earl Russell, it must be said that it is hard to see, in the peculiar circumstances of the country, what other course was open to Pitt except to divide the Provinces. A Whig will admit that a people has a right to choose its own form of government. It would, therefore, have been unjust to deny this right to the French Canadians.

# CHAPTER XXIII.

THE FIRST PARLIAMENT OF UPPER CANADA.—ABOLITION OF
NEGRO SLAVERY.

In the month of August, 1791, the King, by an Order in Council, defined the division line of the new Provinces of Upper and Lower Canada.* On the 18th of November, 1791, Lieutenant-Governor Clarke, at Quebec, issued a Proclamation announcing that, on the 26th of December following, the Constitutional Act should come into operation in the new Provinces of Upper and Lower Canada. On the 18th of September, 1792, the pioneer Parliament of Upper Canada, numbering altogether sixteen members, assembled at Newark, now Niagara. The annals of the North American continent present no incident, in the momentous science of government, to surpass, in the elements of political faith, hope and heroism, the opening of the first Parliament of the Western Province.

* The line, which remains unchanged, is as follows :—" Commencing at a stone boundary on the north bank of Lake St. Francis, at the cove west of the Point au Baudet, in the limit between the township of Lancaster and the seigniory of New Longueil ; running along the said limit in the direction of north, thirty-four degrees west, to the westernmost angle of the said seigniory of New Longueil ; thence along the north-west boundary of the seigniory of Vaudreuil, running north, twenty-five degrees east, until it strikes the Ottawa River ; to ascend the said river into Lake Temiscaming ; and from the head of the said lake, by a line drawn due north until it strikes the boundary line of Hudson's Bay ; including all the territory to the westward and southward of the said line, to the utmost extent of the country commonly called or known by the name of Canada."

The members had been summoned by Lieutenant-Governor Simcoe, foster-father of Upper Canada, an administrator who combined the rare qualities of statesman and soldier. The Parliament assembled in a hut, within the booming of the thunders of the Cataract. South of them and behind them, was a dissevered and an unsympathising people. West, east and north of them was the scowling and unknown wilderness repellent, and terrible in the majesty of its mystery. But those sixteen men were not appalled by these things. In their minds was the kindly memory of the Mother Land ever before them, a benign and visible presence. With that aptitude for government hereditary in the Island Races, they at once addressed themselves to deal with the pressing problems of the hour. They were no visionaries, nor drones, but earnest, laborious men ; British Islanders in their love of liberty and of ancestral precedent ; Spartans in their endurance and in their simplicity. Like the Athenian statesman, if they could not play upon the lute, they could teach how small communities might become great.

It is not the intention of this work to anticipate what may be part of a task hereafter ; which task may be to exhibit in a complete picture the legislation of Upper Canada. But it is only just to notice, in this place, a few of the efforts of our earliest law-makers. Their first proceeding was to repeal that part of the Quebec Bill which provided "that in all matters of controversy, relative to property and civil rights, resort should be had to the laws of Canada." They declared that this provivision was "manifestly and avowedly intended for the accommodation of His Majesty's Canadian subjects." But, since the passing of the Quebec Bill, "that part of the late Province of Quebec now comprehended within the Province of Upper Canada, having become inhabited principally by British subjects . . unaccustomed to the laws of Canada," it was inexpedient that the aforesaid provision "should be continued in this Province." Therefore, " by the King's Most Excellent Majesty, by and with the advice and consent of the Legislative Council and Assembly of the Province of Upper Canada," the provision was repealed. It was further enacted, that "the authority of the said laws of Canada, and every part thereof, as forming a rule of decision in all matters of controversy relative to property and civil rights, shall be annulled, made void and abolished throughout this Province." It was provided, however, that the repeal of the clause should not affect claims on real property, or contracts or securities already executed.

The Act further declared, that from and after the day of its passing,* " in all matters of controversy relative to property and civil rights, resort shall be had to the laws of England, as the rule for the decision of the same." But it was forbidden to make alteration in the existing provisions respecting ecclesiastical rights or dues within the Province, or to introduce any of the laws of England respecting the maintenance of the poor, or respecting bankrupts.

* Oct. 15, 1792.

The second Act of this first session was to establish trials by jury. The preamble has the true ring and stamp of the Constitutional Races :—" Whereas the trial by jury has been long established and approved in our mother country, and is one of the chief benefits to be attained by a free Constitution." Then it was enacted that, after the first of December in the same year, all issues of fact were to be determined by the verdict of twelve jurors, " conformably to the law and custom of England." The proceedings of the first Parliament were satisfactory to Lieutenant-Governor Simcoe, as was shown in his despatches to the Colonial Secretary.*

The second session of the Parliament of Upper Canada, convoked at Newark on the 31st May, 1793, was memorable on account of stamping with the seal of law the noble principle of liberty for the enslaved African. In 1709, the poison of negro slavery was in pestilent flow through the social system of French Canada ; for in that year it had been officially recognised by an edict of the Intendant. By the 47th Article of the Capitulation, the French Canadians were permitted to retain their slaves.

But Upper Canada was determined that human slavery should form no part of her social superstructure. And so, in 1793, her Parliament, the first Legislative Body in the Empire to lift up an authoritative hand against negro bondage, pronounced for evermore the doom of the

* See Dr. Canniff's "Settlement of Upper Canada," p. 637—a valuable and patriotic work.

accursed thing. This Act was the first ennobling utterance of a Voice that has ever since raised itself high, loud and forceful at every epoch in our history when right and liberty needed a pleader or a champion. This Parliament, at a time when settlers were few, when labour was a thing of paramount need, when necessity and avarice clamoured to the baser feelings of human nature with a might that to most men would have proved irresistible, passed an Act "To prevent the further introduction of slaves, and to limit the term of contracts for servitude within this Province."

The preamble opens with this honourable and exalted declaration:—"Whereas it is unjust that a people who enjoy freedom by law, should encourage the introduction of slaves; and whereas it is highly expedient to abolish slavery in this Province, so far as the same may gradually be done without violating private property."* Then follows a series of well-considered enactments to carry out this beneficent legislation.† There was declared to

* See "Statutes of Upper Can., 1791-1831," pp. 41, 42.
† Here are the names of these philanthropists and statesmen of the wilderness—the first on the bead-roll of Upper Canadian worthies:—

ROBERT GRAY, Solicitor-General, and principal promoter of the Act of Emancipation.

| | |
|---|---|
| JOHN MCDONNELL. | HUGH MCDONNELL. |
| JOSHUA BOOTH. | BENJAMIN PAWLING. |
| * * * BABY. | NATHANIEL PETTIT. |
| ALEXANDER CAMPBELL. | DAVID WM. SMITH. |
| PETER VAN ALSTINE. | HAZLETON SPENCER. |
| JEREMIAH FRENCH. | ISAAC SWAZY. |
| EPHRAIM JONES. | * * * YOUNG. |
| WILLIAM MOCOMB. | JOHN WHITE. |

—Dr. Canniff, pp. 534-573.

be repealed so much of an Imperial Act passed in 1790,* "as may enable the Governor or Lieut.-Governor of this Province, heretofore parcel of His Majesty's Province of Quebec, to grant a licence for importing into the same any negro or negroes." The Act then proceeded to define the means by which the negro slavery which had been imported into Upper Canada should be for ever extinguished within the territory of the Western Province.

The object of the Imperial Act of 1790, the most repulsive provision of which the Fathers of Upper Canadian liberty nobly and daringly abolished, was to attract immigration from the United States "to the Bahama, or Bermuda, or Somers Islands, or to any part of the Province of Quebec or Nova Scotia, or any of the territories belonging to His Majesty in North America." The Act made it lawful for any person emigrating from the United States to any of the above-mentioned countries—having first obtained a licence from the Governor or Lieut.-Governor for that purpose—"to import into the same, in British ships owned by His Majesty's subjects, and navigated according to law, any negroes, household furniture, . . . free of duty."

The Legislature of Lower Canada refused to follow the noble example set by its compeer of the Upper Province in vindication of the natural rights of man. But the British Bench came forward to do what the law-makers

* This Act, 30th George III. cap.   , was entitled "An Act for Encouraging new Settlers in His Majesty's Colonies and Plantations in America."

of Lower Canada ought to have been proud to perform. In Montreal, in 1803, in the city where, at the time, mercantile avarice choked the pleadings of human nature, and struggled to make slavery perpetual, Chief Justice Osgoode declared negro bondage to be at variance with the laws of the country. And, in so doing, he gave liberty to the slaves of Lower Canada.*

As Upper Canada began, so, as a rule, whenever, in times past, her people were permitted to act through the Legislature, has she continued. In every movement forward, Upper Canada has been the Vanguard Province. And now, at the present hour, she is reaping the rich rewards of her principle of action in the Past, which was this—to reverence whatever is noble and valuable in the Old ; to welcome whatever is excellent in the New.

* See Dr. Canniff, pp. 570-578, for a highly interesting account of slavery in Canada.

# CHAPTER XXIV.

### THE GIFT OF RELIGIOUS LIBERTY TO CANADA.

To the world, to humanity, to a principle of sublime import, the British Conquest brought a boon never, until that time, presented to Canada. This boon was the bestowal and establishment of religious liberty. Heretofore in our history, this momentous event had achieved no recognition.

A few years following the last successful attempt of France to colonize Canada, and while the seventeenth century was yet young, the Court of France gave stringent orders that the Huguenots should be prevented from entering the Province.* The historian, cited below, avers that, during the first twenty years of the Colony, it was observed that certain of the Huguenots, who had taken part in the work of founding New France, cherished a marked preference for England. In reference to this assertion, it is necessary to observe that the Huguenot side of the story is wanting. There was no one to place on record the counter-statement of these persecuted French Christians, had the charge been made to their faces; nor, had they made a denial, would it have been accepted by their enemies at the Court and in the Colony. These Huguenots, with all their faults, were the lights,

---

\* See Abbé Ferland's "Cours d'Histoire du Canada,"; vol. i. pp. 168, 169.

I

the thinkers and the workers of France. Might they not have been the same in Canada ? In the New England Colonies, where they were welcomed, they left the deep and permanent impress of their moral and civic excellence.* To their mother country, which so cruelly persecuted and banished them, they left only a memory. But this memory, like an incense to liberty, floats upward from dungeons, from scaffolds, from blazing homes and houses of prayer : it soars above the poison vapours of the history of Monarchical France : it ascends and purifies, remaining for the after ages a memorial of heroism and suffering for conscience sake, a perpetual protest against religious persecution. †

The world owes it to Great Britain that her conquest of Canada opened, through the jungle and wilderness of intolerance, the broad and beneficent pathways of religious liberty.

The Conquest is a matter about which the Canadians of the present day may speak without prejudice or bitterness. The ancestors of both races share in a common renown. The victory of the one was untarnished; the defeat of the other was full of more of the elements of

* See M. Chas. Weiss' "History of the French Protestant Refugees," vol. ii. pp. 284-333.

† The historian already quoted treats this grand question of religious liberty in a manner which is at once evasive and equivocal. He says :—" Quelles que soient les opinions qu'on puisse entretenir sur l'article de la tolerance religieuse, il faut avouer que l'exclusion des Huguenots a eu pour effet de procurer plus de liaison entre les differents elements de la societé Canadienne, et d'empêcher de graves divisions à l'intérieur."—" Cours d'Histoire," vol. i, p. 275.

heroism than are to be found in many triumphs. The sudden extinction of the French power in Canada was naturally, for many a year, a subject on which a gallant race could not be expected to dwell with pleasurable remembrance. But this feeling, soothed by the anodynes of time and justice, has long since passed away. It cannot be denied, in the light of experience, that, unwelcome as may have been the rule of Britain at first, that rule was eventually the best for Canada.

Montcalm may be accepted as one of the most single-minded and earnest men that ever represented France on the American continent. Yet he could write :—" Let us beware how we allow the establishment of manufactures in Canada ; she would become proud and mutinous like the English (Colonies). So long as France is a nursery to Canada, let not the Canadians be allowed to trade, but kept to their wandering, laborious life with the savages, and to their military exercises. They will be less wealthy, but more brave and more faithful to us. . . England made a great mistake in not taxing these Colonies from the first, even ever so little. If they now attempt it— revolt.*

* See Warburton's "Conquest of Canada," vol. ii. p. 364.

# CHAPTER XXV.

CANADA PAST AND PRESENT.

In no other colony of the Empire has the British Constitution been subjected to the same strain and tension as in Canada. In no other colony has that Constitution had opportunity to prove so well its marvellous plastic power and universal adaptability. The questions of race and faith entered, at the inception of British rule, into the problem of government; entangled it and made it difficult of solution. But these troubles have been met and overcome.

The Constitutional Act was framed with an honest intent. Pitt never contemplated that his measure should be prostituted to the purposes of oppressing the people of Canada. But to these purposes it was debased. Wielding the Act for nearly half a century, a bulwark of Oligarchy, made up of the drift-wood of the Army and manned by the buccaneers of the Law, beat back the people of Upper Canada from the object of their dearest wishes: the prize and native right of self-government. In Lower Canada a British oligarchy opposed itself to the interests and wishes of the French Canadians, and to those of many of its own people. In that Province, furthermore, the malignant element of race antipathies, drawing sustenance from both populations, intensified and embittered the struggle to a degree unknown in Upper Canada. In the two Provinces the Governors sent out from time to time were, for the most part, fascinated by the Official anacondas, fell into their folds and became their prey. The Governors were the puppets and servants of the Oligarchies ; they were ministers to the latter ; the latter were not ministers to them.

The great principle at stake for nearly half a century, the principle which comprised all the others, was this—which was to rule ? the Legislative Assemblies elected by the Commons, or the Legislative and Executive Councils appointed by the Governors ? In all cases these two auxiliaries of the Constitution set themselves, with political malice aforethought, to thwart the efforts of the Assemblies to obtain control of the Provincial revenues.

In 1837 the contest culminated, in Upper Canada, in the rising of a section of the people ; in Lower Canada, in serious rebellion. The Imperial Parliament suspended the Constitution of Lower Canada. A special Council, nominated by the Governor, assumed the place of Parliament. But in the year 1841, the Union Act brought both Provinces together, conferred on them Responsible Government and the full privileges of a free Constitution.

To our Canadian statesmen who represented the wishes of the people, and who, through good report and evil report, loaded with obloquy and blackened with calumnious charges of treason and hostility to the British Constitution, knocked at the door of the Empire until those wishes met with favour and compliance, the Mother Country owes much ; but we owe more. To the wise, just and sympathetic statesmen of Great Britain, who bore with the importunities of Canada, who overlooked much that was hasty and inconsiderate, and who gave us the boon and privilege of Responsible Government,* Canada and the Empire stand indebted for ever. These far-sighted men refused to be frightened from doing right, by the ravings of those who prophesied that a freer measure of self-government would plunge us into the whirlpool of the Republicanism of the United States. This it has not done, and will not do. Canada knows the abyss; shrinks back from it; will resist to the death being driven into it.

Canada feels she enjoys a fuller measure of liberty than any country in the world, not even excepting the land in whose Constitutional glories we are proud to be participants. In Ontario, the greatest Province of the Confederation, a Municipal System, without parallel for the scope it affords for local liberty, brings home the benefits of domestic self-government to every community of 750 individuals. But our people are an educated people. By their intelligence they won their privileges; with their intelligence they can develop and preserve them. Political ignorance could work no such system as ours, nor handle it with safety or advantage.

In the year 1864 was exemplified the truth of the prophecy of Pitt in 1791, That, if the two Provinces were represented in the one Parliament, and parties were equally balanced, legislation might become an impossi-

* In 1841.

bility. The Union Act of 1841 gave to Upper and Lower Canada an equal number of representatives. Between this period and 1864, the population of Upper Canada had gained upon and far exceeded that of Lower Canada. To the demand of the Upper Province for increased representation, the Lower Province persistently refused to accede. Parties were in such critical equipoise, that, in 1864, one vote defeated a Conservative Government.

It was now seen that the Constitution would have to undergo an organic change. A Federal system was adopted; the one under which we now live and thrive, and promise still more to flourish. To bring about the new form of Government, Sir John A. Macdonald, the leader of the Conservative Party, and the Hon. George Brown, the leader of the Liberal Party—the Party which demanded for Upper Canada Parliamentary representation based on the principle of population, magnanimously resolved to sink their political differences; and, moved by a common patriotic impulse, entered into a union of political peace. The Federal system has been in operation since 1867, and every day adds proof to its excellence.

In a country like Canada, peopled by diverse races, a Federal Government is the one under which may best be preserved that healthy national individualism which, in its ennobling rivalry, stimulates to its full extent the action of those vital political and social forces that give to a State vigour, freshness and valiant self-reliance. Our past history proves that it would be unjust and impossible to endeavour to reduce our nationa elements to a dead and waveless level. And our past history also teaches to those in power this lesson : That, to concede in season and in justice is to disarm discontent and danger ; is to satisfy and to retain.

END VOLUME I.

# INDEX.

## CHAPTER I.

|  | PAGE |
|---|---|
| Capitulation of Canada ... ... ... ... | 9 |
| Free exercise of Roman Catholic Religion granted... | 10 |
| Military Rule... ... ... ... ... ... | 10 |
| Treaty of Paris. Peace between Great Britain and France ... ... ... ... ... ... | 10 |
| French King cedes Canada ... ... ... | 10-11 |
| English King grants, conditionally, liberty of Roman Catholic Religion ... ... ... ... | 11 |
| Canadian Seigniors and Vassals ... ... ... | 11 |
| Feudal prerogatives of the Seigniors ... ... | 11 |
| Vassals oppressed by King and Seignior ... ... | 12 |
| Conquest brings relief to the Vassals ... | 12-13 |
| Population, noble and plebeian, at the Conquest ... | 13 |
| Antipathy between Vassal and Seignior ... ... | 13 |
| French Nobility in Canada ... ... ... ... | 14 |
| The Conquest causes emigration of the French Nobility ... ... ... ... ... ... | 15 |

## CHAPTER II.

Royal Proclamation introduces laws of England ... 16

146 INDEX.

|   | PAGE |
|---|---|
| Quebec erected into a Province; boundaries defined | 16 |
| King promises, under conditions, a House of Assembly | 16-17 |
| Royal protection for laws of England | 17 |
| Oaths of Members of future Assembly | 17 |
| A Council appointed | 17 |
| Constitutional question : "Great Seal of Great Britain" v. "Royal Signet and Sign Manual" | 17-18 |
| Legislative powers of the Council | 18 |
| Canadian Noblesse dislike laws of England | 18-19 |
| Number of British and French in Canada in 1770 | 19 |
| Royal promise as to House of Assembly unfulfilled. Disappointment of British Colonists | 20 |

## CHAPTER III.

| British Colonists petition for House of Assembly | 22 |
|---|---|
| British Ministry unfavourable to Petition | 23 |
| Sacrifice demanded of British Colonists to gain House of Assembly | 23 |
| French Canadian Seigniorial and Legal classes petition | 24 |
| They prefer military government with French laws to civil government with English laws | 25 |
| British Ministers on the point of re-enacting the Criminal Law of France (*Note*) | 25 |

INDEX. 147

## CHAPTER IV.

PAGE

Change of Government for Canada. The Quebec Bill ... ... ... ... ... ... 27
Bill founded on French Petition. British Petition disregarded ... ... ... ... ... 27
Indecent haste of British Ministry ... ... ... 28
Burke, Fox, Barré oppose Bill ... ... ... 28
Lord North and Cabinet refuse concessions to British Colonists ... ... ... ... ... 28
*Habeas corpus* for Canada voted down by Ministers.. 29
Earl of Chatham protests against Bill. It passes ... 30
Lord Mayor of London and Common Council attempt to petition King... ... ... ... ... 30
King assents to Bill. His opinion of measure ... 31
Real intent of Ministers. Solicitor-General Wedderburne's speech ... ... ... ... 32
Object of Bill, purposely to discourage British settlement ... ... ... ... ... ... 32
Analysis and substance of Bill ... ... ... 32
Injustice to British Colonists within and beyond Canada ... ... ... ... ... ... 36

## CHAPTER V.

Canada protests against the Quebec Bill. ... ... 37
Petition against Bill sent to the King ... ... 37
Evil results of Bill enumerated ... ... ... 38
Petition to Lords ... ... ... ... ... 38

148                    INDEX.

|                                                                 | PAGE |
|---|---|
| Lords disregard Petition and refuse to repeal Bill ... | 39 |
| Petition to Commons... ... ... ... ... | 39 |
| Repeal of Quebec Bill moved in Commons ... | 41 |
| Lord North threatens to arm Roman Catholics of Canada against Thirteen Colonies ... ... | 41 |
| Charles James Fox's charge against Lord North ... | 41 |
| Commons refuse to repeal Bill ... ... ... | 41 |
| French Canadian majority displeased with Bill ... | 42 |
| They offer to join British in opposition; are withheld by their superiors ... ... ... | 42 |
| The Thirteen Colonies incensed against Bill ... | 43 |
| Congress address people of Great Britain, complaining of Bill ... ... ... ... ... | 44 |

## CHAPTER VI.

| | |
|---|---|
| British Ministry achieve their object; they gain over clergy and seigniors ... ... ... | 46 |
| First taxes imposed by Britain since Conquest | ..46-47 |
| Composition of Legislative Council... ... ... | 47 |
| Address of Congress to inhabitants of Quebec ... | 48 |
| Serious result of address on Canadian population ... | 49 |
| Congress attempt to deceive Canada ... ... | 50 |
| Martial Law proclaimed; Militia called out ... | 51 |
| Malign influence of Quebec Bill on defence of Province ... ... ... ... ... | 51-52 |

## CHAPTER VII.

Hostility of Peasants to Quebec Bill and Seigniors    53

INDEX. 149
PAGE

Peasants rebel against Seigniors ... ... 53-55
Reason of revolt of Peasants ... ... ... 55
Population of the towns detest Quebec Bill ... 56
French Canadian Militia make Governor promise to
    use his efforts for its repeal ... ... ... 56

## CHAPTER VIII.

Status of Roman Catholic Church in Canada ... 57
Penal laws of British Islands do not extend to Colo-
    nies ... ... .. ... ... ... 57
Mgr. Briand elected Bishop of Quebec ... ... 58
King consents that Bishop should be invested by the
    Pope ... ... ... ... .. ... 58
High-handed proceedings of Bishop towards his
    flock ... ... ... ... ... ... 59
He exhorts his people to oppose American invaders 59
Threatens with excommunication those who refuse 59-60
The people disobey and satirize the Bishop... 60-61

## CHAPTER IX.

Perilous situation of Canada ... ... ... 62
The Governor deceived in his Militia ... ... 62
French Canadians assist Americans ... ... 62
Some of British Colonists sympathise with Ameri-
    cans ... .. ... ... ... ... 63
General Montgomery takes possession of Montreal 63

150  INDEX.

|  | PAGE |
|---|---|
| The Americans hold all Canada, except Quebec | 63-64 |
| Montgomery assaults Quebec. His death. Failure of the invasion ... ... ... ... ... | 64 |

## CHAPTER X.

Colonial misgovernment ... ... ... ... 66
Responsibility of Colonial authorities for maladministration. ... ... ... ... ... 66
British Ministers kept in ignorance of Canadian grievances ... ... ... ... ... 67
Canadian Governors deceived by Canadian Oligarchies ... ... ... ... ... ... 67
Quebec Bill based upon partial information... ... 67
British Ministry desire to mitigate some evils of the Bill ... ... ... ... ... ... 68
*Habeas Corpus* about to be re-established in Canada 68
French Canadian Legislative Councillors oppose it 68-69
American Invasion assists to postpone *Habeas Corpus* ... ... ... ... ... ... 69

## CHAPTER XI.

Introduction of English laws by Royal Proclamation of 1764 ... ... .. ... ... .. 70
Constitutional argument against introduction of English laws ... ... ... ... 70-71
Nature of the supplanted French laws ... ... 71

INDEX. 151

PAGE

Judges—sessions of courts—power of appeal—Supreme Council ... ... ... ... ... 71
Composition of Supreme Council ; its powers 71-72
Attorneys for the King ; their duties ... ... 72
Court of the Intendant; its jurisdiction .. ... 73

## CHAPTER XII.

The laws of inheritance. No primogeniture ... 74
Restraints on the Seigniors as to subdivisions of inheritance. ... ... ... ... ... 74
Restraints in the case of the Peasants ... ... 75
Defect of the French jurisprudence ... ... 75
Re-establishment of the French civil laws ... ... 76

## CHAPTER XIII.

Feudal tenure ; Peasant servitudes... ... ... 77
Tenure by which the Seigniors held of the King ... 77
Peasant tenures ; burdens and restraints ... ... 78
Redeeming feature of the Seigniorial system ... 79
Immense territorial grants to the Seigniors ... 80
King of England endeavours to perpetuate feudal system in future Province of Upper Canada 80-81

## CHAPTER XIV.

Canadian Reign of Terror ... ... ... ... 82
Despotic Character of Legislative Council ... ... 82

|  | PAGE |
|---|---|
| Military Tyranny established by Council | 83 |
| Commercial Code of England introduced; Courts of Oyer and Terminer established | 83 |
| Tyranny of Governor Haldimand | 84 |
| Council vote down introduction of the Laws of England | 85 |
| Military arrests; their injustice | 85 |
| Robbery of Mails by Government | 85-86 |

## CHAPTER XV.

| Peace between Great Britain and the United States | 87 |
|---|---|
| Liberation of Canadian Political prisoners | 87 |
| Territorial gluttony of United States | 87 |
| British Ministry wish to revive *Habeas Corpus* | 87-88 |
| Legislative Council make delays | 88 |
| *Habeas Corpus* wrung from the Council | 8 |

## CHAPTER XVI.

| British and French petition Home Government for Constitutional changes | 89 |
|---|---|
| Legislative Council resist petition | 89 |
| Lord Sidney's unjust opinion of petitioners | 89 |
| British Ministry at length condescend to notice Canada | 90 |
| Mr. Grenville transmits to Canada scheme of a Constitution | 90 |
| Wretched social condition of the Province | 91 |
| Disgraceful state of the Judiciary | 91 |

INDEX. 153

## CHAPTER XVII.

|  | PAGE |
|---|---|
| The Nation-Builders of Upper Canada | 93 |
| The Loyalists of the Thirteen Colonies | 93 |
| Persecution of the Loyalists | 94 |
| They take refuge in Western Canada | 94 |
| Imperial favours conferred on the exiles | 95 |
| Political opinions of the Loyalists | 95 |
| They protest against feudal tenures | 96 |
| They claim a Parliament of their own | 96 |

## CHAPTER XVIII.

| Canada in the British Parliament | 97 |
|---|---|
| King's Message; Division of the Province; A Protestant Clergy | 97 |
| William Pitt's motion based on Message | 97-98 |
| He introduces a Bill to settle future Government of Canada | 98 |
| Provisions of the new Bill | 98-100 |
| Charles James Fox on the Measure. Favours self-Government for Canada | 100 |

## CHAPTER XIX.

| British Merchants of Quebec oppose Constitutional Act | 102 |
|---|---|
| Mr. Lymburner, their agent, heard at bar of the Commons | 102 |
| He depicts juridical confusion of Quebec | 103 |

K

154   INDEX.

PAGE

Opposes desire of Western Loyalists for division of
  Province ... ... ... ... ... 103
Protests against aristocratic enactments of the Act 104
Points out defect in representation of American
  Colonies ... ... ... ... ... 105
Entreats for postponement of payment of Provincial
  Civil List ... ... ... ... 105-106
Makes certain requests on behalf of his constituents 106

CHAPTER XX.

Fox and Pitt on the New Constitution ... ... 107
Fox opposes the limited representation proposed ... 107
He objects to Septennial Parliaments for Canada ... 108
Disapproves of excessive electoral qualification ... 108
Contends against introduction of hereditary powers
  and honours in Canada ... ... 108-109
Combats reservation of lands for ecclesiastics 109-110
Comments unfavourably on proposed division of
  Quebec ... ... ... ... ... 110-111
Shows how Britain may retain Canada ... ... 111
Present Act only shadow of British Constitution ... 111
Pitt's doubts as to greater numerical representation 112
He defends Septennial Parliaments ... ... 112
Contends for a non-elective Legislative Council ... 113
Upholds ecclesiastical land reserves; and division
  of Province ... ... ... ... ... 113
Points out inconvenience of a single House of Assembly ... .. .. ... ... ... 114

INDEX. 155

PAGE

Fox moves to abolish hereditary principle. Negatived ... ... ... ... ... ... 114
Moves for increased representation for Lower Canada. Negatived; Bill passed ... ... 114-115

## CHAPTER XXI.

The Constitutional Act of 1791 ... ... ... 116
Provisions of the Act repealed by Union Act of 1841 119
Tithes for a Protestant Clergy (abolished in Upper Canada) ... ... ... ... ... ... 120
Lands for a Protestant Clergy (subsequent Imperial and Provincial restrictions) ... ... ... 121
Provincial Legislation prescribed as to ecclesiastical lands (subsequent freedom of Legislation) ... 122
Free land tenures for Upper Canada ... ... 122
British Parliament renounce the right of internal taxation in Canada ... ... ... 123-124
*Habeas Corpus* not guaranteed in the Act. How it became law ... ... ... ... ... 125

## CHAPTER XXII.

Defects of the Constitutional Act ... ... ... 126
Fox's political predictions ... ... ... 126
Pitt's political foresight ... ... ... 126-127
Legislative Assemblies shorn of their power ... 128
Failure of the Act to establish a Canadian Aristocracy ... ... ... ... ... ... 128

|                                                      | PAGE |
|------------------------------------------------------|------|
| Earl Russell on the Constitutional Act ...           | 128-129 |
| Inconsistency of his position ...  ...  ...          | 129  |

## CHAPTER XXIII.

| | |
|---|---|
| First Parliament of Upper Canada ... ... | 130 |
| They repeal " civil rights " clause of Quebec Bill ... | 131 |
| English laws made the rule of decision ... ... | 131 |
| Poor laws and bankrupt laws of England excluded | 131 |
| Trials by Jury established ... ... ... ... | 133 |
| Negro slavery in French Canada ... ... ... | 133 |
| Upper Canada, the first member of the Empire to abolish negro slavery ... ... ... | 133-134 |
| Legislature of Upper Canada repeal Imperial Act of 1790, authorizing importation of negroes ... | 135 |
| Lower Canada Legislature refuse to follow example of Upper Canada ... ... ... | 135-136 |
| Chief Justice Osgoode, in Lower Canada, in 1803, decides against negro slavery ... ... ... | 136 |

## CHAPTER XXIV.

| | |
|---|---|
| The Conquest confers religious liberty on Canada ... | 137 |
| The Huguenots excluded in the early days of French Colonization ... ... ... ... ... | 137 |
| Charges made against the Huguenots ... ... | 137 |
| New England welcomes the Huguenots and profits by them ... ... ... ... ... ... | 138 |
| Feelings excited by the Conquest no longer exist | 138-139 |

INDEX. 157

Montcalm's singular opinions as to the Government
of French Canada ... ... ... ... 139

## CHAPTER XXV.

Canada past and present ... ... ... ... 140
Strain on the British Constitution in Canada ... 140
Perversion and debasement of the Constitutional
Act ... ... ... ... ... ... 140
Canadian Oligarchies and Canadian Governors 140-141
Principle for which Legislative Assemblies con-
tended ... ... ... ... ... ... 141
Opposition of Legislative Councils—Outbreak of
1837 ... ... ... ... ... ... 141
Union of Upper and Lower Canada, 1841. Respon-
sible Government conceded ... ... ... 141
Canadian and British Statesmen : efforts of former ;
magnanimity of latter ... ... ... 141-142
False prophets. United States Republicanism
spurned in Canada ... ... ... ... 142
Ontario—Comprehensiveness of her local liberties.
Her Municipal Institutions ... ... ... 142
Pitt's prediction fulfilled in 1864 ... ... ... 142
Failure of the Union Act of 1841 ... ... ... 143
Sir John A. Macdonald and Hon. George Brown,
opposing Party leaders ... ... ... ... 143
They unite to originate a New Constitution ... 143
Our Federal system. Its advantages in a country of
diverse races ... ... ... ... 143-144

www.ingramcontent.com/pod-product-compliance
Lightning Source LLC
Chambersburg PA
CBHW030312170426
43202CB00009B/979